What People Are Saying About

Quakers and Chocolate

A must read for anyone interested in the history of chocolate. Helen Holt takes us through the origins of chocolate and the role that Quakers played in its production, its development and in making it the well-loved treat we know today. While she touches on the historical and modern-day ethical issues involved in chocolate production, her focus is on the families involved in chocolate production and the way in which they brought their Quaker values into their businesses, setting an example that businesses today would do well to follow.
Kate McNally, judge for the International Chocolate Awards

In this fascinating book, Helen Holt shows us how three Quaker families unlocked the cocoa bean to create the 'food of the gods' and how their wealth was handed on in service to others. Devotion to the search for the perfect recipe was, at times, an obsession, as these pioneer chocolatiers experimented with new-fangled processes and machines until they created the chocolates we know and love today. The profits were not all spent on their families but were used to improve the working and living conditions of their employees and to challenge injustice more widely. Together, these stories reveal a passion for innovation and a concern for all that grew out of Quaker beliefs in justice, compassion, and generosity.
Ruth Tod, author of *Exploring Isaac Penington*

T0348654

Quakers and Chocolate

Quakers and Chocolate

Helen Holt

CHRISTIAN ALTERNATIVE
BOOKS

London, UK
Washington, DC, USA

CollectiveInk

First published by Christian Alternative Books, 2025
Christian Alternative Books is an imprint of Collective Ink Ltd.,
Unit 11, Shepperton House, 89 Shepperton Road, London, N1 3DF
office@collectiveinkbooks.com
www.collectiveinkbooks.com
www.christian-alternative.com

For distributor details and how to order please visit the 'Ordering' section on our website.

Text copyright: Helen Holt 2023

ISBN: 978 1 80341 620 5
978 1 80341 714 1 (ebook)
Library of Congress Control Number: 2023949853

All rights reserved. Except for brief quotations in critical articles or reviews, no part of this
book may be reproduced in any manner without prior written permission from the publishers.

The rights of Helen Holt as author have been asserted in accordance with
the Copyright, Designs and Patents Act 1988.

A CIP catalogue record for this book is available from the British Library.

Design: Lapiz Digital Services

UK: Printed and bound by CPI Group (UK) Ltd, Croydon, CR0 4YY
Printed in North America by CPI GPS partners

We operate a distinctive and ethical publishing philosophy in
all areas of our business, from our global network of authors to
production and worldwide distribution.

Contents

Other Titles by This Author

Rufus Jones and the Presence of God
(Christian Alternative Books, 2023)
ISBN 978-1-80341-342-6

Quakers and Science
(Christian Alternative Books, 2023)
ISBN 978-1-80341-139-2

Mysticism and the Inner Light
in the Thought of Rufus Jones, Quaker
(Brill, 2022)
ISSN 1566-208X

Introduction

In 1753, the Swedish naturalist Carl von Linnaeus named the curious-looking cacoa tree *Theobroma cacoa*, with *Theobroma* deriving from the Greek for 'food of the gods'. Also in 1753, the Bristol Quaker Joseph Fry opened an apothecary and a few years later started selling cocoa, extolling it for its health benefits. In a little over a century, the Fry family and their fellow Quakers—the Rowntrees in York and the Cadburys in Birmingham—would be instrumental in transforming the food of the gods into the food of the masses.[1]

The lives of these Quaker chocolatiers were shaped by their firm belief that God could be found within all people and by an associated long-standing tradition of social reform. These twin aspects of Quakerism—looking inwards and looking outwards—shaped how they ran their businesses and how they gained and spent their vast fortunes. Both the Cadburys and the Rowntrees built factories in the countryside, claiming that this would allow their employees to develop all that was best within them. They provided free access to doctors and dentists, numerous social opportunities from camera clubs to cricket pitches, continuing education for their young workforce, and, in an age when the spectre of the workhouse haunted the elderly, old age pensions. They also built villages for their employees and others, aiming to provide an alternative to crowded, unsanitary slums in the form of pleasant, affordable houses with large gardens. These Quakers have sometimes been accused of paternalism, but they saw their employees as colleagues, and in a society without state pensions, sick pay, and the NHS, the benefits they conferred were surely a godsend to many.

Quakers weren't the only ones involved in manufacturing chocolate in the nineteenth century of course. Today's familiar brands include those started by Joseph Terry in York, Henri

1

Nestlé and Rodolphe Lindt in Switzerland, and Milton Hershey in America. Nor were Quakers the only industrialists to challenge the status quo when it came to the welfare of their employees. Robert Owen (1771–1858) thought all religions were false and in later life turned to spiritualism. He blazed a trail at New Lanark for his textile workers, improving factory conditions and arguing that the current structure of society repressed the higher qualities of human nature. Milton Hershey (1857–1945) was from a Mennonite family and married a Catholic. He established the Hershey Industrial School for orphans and built a flamboyant town near his chocolate works on a grand scale: there were wide boulevards, landscaped gardens, a miniature railroad, and even a zoo.

It is interesting to ask, then, how the faith and religious concerns of these three Quaker chocolate families flavoured their business decisions and social enterprises. What, if anything, did they do differently because they were Quakers? The answer regarding the starting point of their businesses is clear enough. For the first few centuries of their existence, Quakers were severely constrained in their choice of career. As non-conformists they were excluded from studying at Oxford and Cambridge until the mid-nineteenth century, they were restricted in what they could do as lawyers because of their refusal to swear oaths (the implication being that an oath implied a double standard of truth-telling), and they refused to enter the armed forces because of their stance against war. As a result, many Quakers opted for a career in industry, business, or shopkeeping, where they gained a reputation for hard work and integrity. You could send a child to a Quaker shop, confident that they would not be cheated. The first generation of all our chocolate dynasties started out as shopkeepers before moving into manufacturing. Furthermore, many Quakers were involved in the Adult School movement, which gave them an intimate knowledge of the problems caused by poverty, slums, and illiteracy. Both George Cadbury (1839–1922) and Joseph Rowntree (1836–1925) taught weekly classes for decades and credited the experience with informing their commitment to improving conditions for their employees.

Individuals naturally experience their faith in different ways and have different personalities, however, so we should expect some differences in the ways that these Quaker chocolatiers ran their businesses. George Cadbury took over his father's ailing business in his early twenties, aided by his brother Richard. He was driven, ambitious, thrived on struggle, embraced risk, and was open about his beliefs. Joseph Rowntree entered the chocolate business reluctantly, feeling he needed to bail out his likeable but easily distracted brother Henry, whose chocolate enterprise was facing bankruptcy. He was studious, devoted a huge amount of time and effort to collecting statistics on poverty, often proceeded cautiously, and rarely talked about his personal faith. Both George and Joseph, however, firmly believed that the purpose of money was to improve conditions for others and warned of the dangers of inherited wealth. As a consequence, both gave away significant portions of their fortunes.

While all three Quaker chocolate businesses passed to the sons and grandsons of their founders, some descendants stand out for their accomplishments outside of the chocolate factory. Beatrice Boeke (née Cadbury; 1884–1976) was the niece of George Cadbury. Despite, or perhaps because of, her privileged upbringing, she denounced capitalism and tried to give away her fortune. She and her Dutch husband also refused to pay taxes because they objected to funding the military. It was a stance that would lead to spells in prison and a summer spent homeless. John Wilhelm Rowntree (1868–1905) was the son of Joseph Rowntree and widely respected as an inspirational Quaker reformer. He spear-headed the idea that formulations of faith must change to incorporate knowledge gained from science and biblical criticism, all the while living with a disease that was slowly robbing him of his sight and that would contribute to his premature death.

This short book looks at the history of chocolate and at some of the members of the Quaker chocolate dynasties. The first chapter takes a bird's eye view of the history of chocolate, from its often opulent and occasionally gruesome beginnings in the ancient civilizations of Mesoamerica to its journey into Europe through monks, medics, and nobles. The Quakers enter the story in the second chapter, as they battle against impending bankruptcy, get to grips with the latest technology, strive to give their employees a physically and spiritually healthy life, and ultimately see the family businesses they grew bought by global food giants. In the next four chapters we'll get to know the four abovementioned Quakers—George Cadbury, Joseph Rowntree, Beatrice Boeke, and John Wilhelm Rowntree—a bit better, looking at how their Quaker faith informed their actions. The final chapter briefly considers the Quaker chocolate legacy in relation to health, ethical issues, and various Joseph Rowntree trusts.

The beliefs of today's Quakers have evolved since the time of the events recounted here. The ties with Christianity have been loosened, with some Quakers now self-identifying as Buddhist Quakers or non-theist Quakers, for example. And today's competitive environment means that businesses often seek profits at the expense of worker welfare. Even so, perhaps these Quaker chocolatiers can inspire us to find creative ways to combine spiritual and business values for the good of all.

Chapter 1

A brief history of chocolate: On gods, monks, and murderers

The cacoa tree is native to the northwest Amazon basin, where it was probably domesticated for its delicious pulp. Humans then likely spread it from Ecuador into the Soconusco region (the southwest corner of the Mexican state of Chiapas and its border with Guatemala), and from there northwards across the Isthmus of Tehuantepec to the Gulf Coast. Although it belongs to the genus *Theobroma* (along with about 20 other species of flowering understory trees), in this particular case *Theopoto*, or drink of the gods, might be a more apt description, as it is only in the last 150 years or so of chocolate's nearly 4000-year history that it has been eaten rather than drunk. It is, however, associated with gods—those of various ancient Mesoamerican cultures.

There is little about the appearance of the tree that would suggest that it might deserve such a divine association. It is small (6–12 m) and spindly, with the trunk and larger branches spouting dimpled rugby-ball-shaped pods in a fruiting pattern known as cauliflory. It is disease-prone (to pod rots, wilts, and fungus-produced witches' broom), pernickety about growing conditions (only bearing fruit within 20 degrees either side of the equator) and requires year-round moisture. Its flowers are pollinated not by iridescent humming birds or exotic insects but by midges, which live in the detritus on the forest floor. Furthermore, the seeds within the pods cannot be eaten straight from the tree but must undergo a four-stage process of fermentation, drying, roasting, and winnowing that can take several weeks.

Figure 1: A cacao tree bearing pods containing the valuable
cacoa beans (public domain)

Research into the history of chocolate is still patchy, but
hints of its earliest use come from the analysis of residues on
pottery. *T. cacoa* is the only Mesoamerican plant that contains
the alkaloid theobromine (with 'theobromine' deriving from
Theobroma), so its presence is a unique marker for the use of
cacao in pre-Columbian artefacts. Radiocarbon dating of pottery
reveals that humans were beginning to drink cacoa products
almost 4000 years ago (although it is not always clear whether
they were drinking chocolate or beer fermented from the pulp
inside the pods). The earliest evidence comes from the Olmecs,
who flourished between about 1500 and 400 BCE in the humid
lowlands of the Mexican Gulf Coast. There, they built massive
earth and clay mounds and pyramids for ceremonial purposes,
and a recent study of an ancient site in San Lorenzo revealed
several hundred vessels with residues of theobromine over a
burial pit that contained the remains of sacrificial victims. The
pots were radiocarbon dated to the beginning of the Olmec
period, and it seems likely that the post-interment celebration
included drinking some form of cacoa.

Slightly more is known about the next period of chocolate's history, that of the Maya of the Yucatan Peninsula, who lived in an area that today includes southeastern Mexico and parts of Guatemala and Belize. Maya civilization thrived in one form or another from about 2000 BCE to CE 1700 (with the Classic Maya period from CE 250 to CE 950). Spouted ceramic jars from northern Belize dating to 600 BCE have been found with traces of theobromine, and it is thought that the spouts were used to pour and blow air into the liquid to create a froth, which is known to have been highly prized by later Mesoamericans: over a millennium later, one beautifully detailed scene on a vase from CE 750 shows a woman elegantly producing froth by pouring chocolate from waist height to a pot on the ground.

There is also a glimpse of the Maya attitude to chocolate in various surviving books, made from long strips of bark-paper. The stunning Madrid Codex dates between 1200 and 1450 and consists mainly of almanacs and horoscopes that were used by priests, but one scene has the phonetic 'kakaw' with a picture of a young god grasping limbs from a cacoa tree, and another depicts four gods piercing their ears with obsidian lances, scattering showers of their blood over cacao pods. The Maya took their cacoa in various forms, as drinks, gruels and powders, to which could be added a wide variety of flavours ranging from chilli to an unknown substance thought to be translated as 'fruity'.

From the tenth to the twelfth century, the Toltecs were the dominant civilization in the central highlands of Mexico, and the regions to the northwest were populated by the Anasazi, who developed the Pueblo culture, living in large communal houses. Pueblo Bonito in the Chaco Canyon of New Mexico is the site of one such stone-built multi-story house, which boasted about 350 rooms and was inhabited from about 850 to 1150. Shards of pottery found there have tested positive for theobromine, and it is thought that cacoa beans (along with copper bells and silver objects) from the south were being traded for Anasazi turquoise, which was valued for its use in decorating wooden masks and shields.

By the beginning of the fourteenth century, Aztec immigrants were living as vassals and serfs for the cultural descendants of the Toltec civilization. But within a century they had brought a large part of Mesoamerica under their sway. Their two main drinks were the alcoholic octli, made from the agave plant, and chocolate. There were strict rules about who could drink alcohol, however, and the penalty for drunkenness was often death. That said, there was some ambivalence about the use of chocolate too. In one cautionary tale, a custodian to the gods who can control his age at will reprimands an imperial delegation of sorcerers who lack his abilities: 'You have become old, you have become tired because of the chocolate you drink and because of the foods you eat. They have harmed and weakened you.'[1] The Aztecs, like many of us today, were undeterred. They drank chocolate cold and, like the Maya, prized the froth. They too added various sweet and savoury spices, including vanilla and dried flowers.

The consumption of chocolate was not for the masses, but was confined to the Aztec elite, marching soldiers, and long-distance merchants: the Elder Moctezuma (who reigned from 1440 to 1468) had decreed that he who did not go to war could not wear cotton, feathers or flowers, smoke, or drink cacoa. Aztec warriors were given ground cacoa made into pellets or wafers (along with maize, ground beans, and dried chillis), and long-distance merchants qualified for cacoa rations because they were often armed and had to travel through dangerous territories. The elite drank chocolate at the end of meals while smoking tubes of tobacco: Moctezuma II (who reigned from about 1502 to 1520) is said to have drunk it from cups of gold, although some sources say the cups were of a more pedestrian calabash. Whatever the cups were made of, there was no shortage of beans—the chronicler Francisco Cervantes de

Salazar reported that the emperor's cacao warehouse contained 40,000 porter-loads of 24,000 beans each, giving a grand total of 960 million.

One notable exception to this restricted access to chocolate was the unfortunate slave who was chosen once a year in Tenochtitlan to impersonate the great god Quetzalcoatl. He was dressed as a god and treated as one for 40 days, then told of his fate and made to perform a dance. If he did not dance with sufficient joy, he was fed a gruesome concoction—chocolate mixed with the blood from knives used in previous sacrifices. The god/slave then became almost unconscious, forgot what he had been told, and continued to dance with gladness, bewitched by the drink.

In 1519, the Spanish Conquistador Hernán Cortés landed in Mexico. The subsequent combination of brutal warfare and European disease decimated the Aztecs, and the Aztec Empire fell. In time, however, Spanish and Aztec culture creolized, and chocolate was taken into the colonial cuisine of New Spain and eventually transplanted to Old Spain and the rest of Europe. Whites took their chocolate hot rather than cold, sweetened it with cane sugar, and frothed it not by pouring but by using a *molinillo*, a grooved wooden beater or swizzle-stick.

Not everyone immediately took to this strange drink. The Jesuit José de Acosta wrote in 1590 that 'It disgusts those who are not used to it, for it has a foam on top, or a scum-like bubbling.... It is a valued drink which the Indians offer to the lords who come or pass through their land. And the Spanish men—and even more the Spanish women—are addicted to the black chocolate'.[2]

One striking example of the extent of the addiction of some Spanish women was recounted by Thomas Gage about his stay in Chiapa Real (now San Cristobel de la Casas) in a book he wrote in 1648. The upper-class white ladies of the town were in the habit of drinking bowls of hot chocolate during Mass, which were brought to them by their Indian maids. The bishop, understandably irritated by the disruption this caused and having failed to talk the ladies out of the practice, eventually took the drastic step of declaring that all who ate or drank in the cathedral would be excommunicated. Undeterred, the ladies found an alternative venue for Mass and continued drinking chocolate. The story might have ended there, but it has a sinister coda. The bishop was given chocolate to drink, soon become ill, and eight days later was dead (having asked God to forgive the perpetrators). It was thought that the chocolate had been poisoned by one of the bishop's pages, who was on intimate terms with one of the chocoholics.

José de Acosta may have disliked drinking cocoa, but his fellow Jesuits found various ways to make money from it. The more conventional way was to sell cacao from the wild trees growing along the Amazon in Brazil, a practice that was mentioned in a report from 1639 and that continued until the 1750s, when measles and smallpox wiped out most of the Indian gatherers. More unconventionally, in 1701 the Spanish flotilla from the Indies arrived in Spain with eight exceptionally heavy crates marked 'Chocolate for the Very Reverend Father General of the Company of Jesus'. The crates did indeed appear to contain substantial blocks of chocolate, but further investigation revealed that this chocolate had a truly golden centre—a finger-thickness of chocolate was coating bars of pure gold. (Sensitive to the fact that all gold was the property of the king and that they could therefore be accused of smuggling, the Jesuits denied having sent the shipment.)

Around the time of the Conquest, cacoa beans were also used as a currency. For a time at least, money really did grow on trees. The sixteenth-century chronicler Francisco Oviedo y Valdés recorded that a rabbit was worth 10 cacoa beans, a slave about 100, and the services of a prostitute 8–10, 'according to how they agree'.

It is possible that chocolate came to Spain for the first time as early as 1544, when Dominican friars took a delegation of Kekchi Maya nobles from Guatemala to visit Prince Philip in Spain, as receptacles of beaten chocolate are included in the list of presents. But it does not seem to have taken hold, and it was the first half of the seventeenth century before it reached the Spanish court, in the form of the hot beverage that had become popular among the Spaniards of Mexico. It was also served in less refined settings — at bullfights and at punishments ordained by the Spanish Inquisition.

The means by which chocolate spread from Spain to the rest of Europe is still ambiguous. The Jesuits were trading in chocolate, and the practice of drinking chocolate might have spread through them and other travelling monks and nuns. It might also have spread through ruling families. One commonly quoted theory is that chocolate arrived in France with Anne of Austria (the daughter of Philip III of Spain) when she was forced into a political marriage with Louis XIII of France in 1615. There is little evidence for this though, and it is more likely that it entered France through yet another route — that of medicine. In France, the Cardinal of Lyon used cocoa as a medicine for his spleen, with one source from 1713 claiming that he heard about the treatment from Spanish monks in France. And in Italy, the Roman physician Paulo Zacchia mentioned it as a drug in a book in 1644. It should, he advises, be taken early in the morning to comfort the stomach.

Even though at this time cacoa had not been made into the chocolate bars we have today, one notable debate that raged in the church for over two and a half centuries was whether cocoa was a food or a drink. It was a question of grave importance for vast numbers of people, because the answer determined whether it could be consumed during fasts such as Lent. The Italian Cardinal Francesco Maria Brancaccio, who in 1664 wrote a short work translated as 'Essay Concerning the Drinking of Chocolate', declared that chocolate, like wine, was one of the necessities of life and could be taken even on fast days. His position was endorsed by a series of popes who were consulted and ruled in its favour. That did not stop many clerics trying to ban it, however: they argued that it was a form of nourishment because a person can subsist on it for quite a long time, especially as it was often mixed with all sorts of ground-up substances. Others who waded into the debate took a commonsense approach — in 1645, the learned Tomás Hurtardo, chair of theology at the University of Seville, declared it to be permissible if water was added, but not eggs or milk.

Cacoa almost made it to England when English buccaneers captured a Spanish ship carrying crates of cacoa beans. In 1579, Thomas Gage described the ensuing tragic mistake: 'When we have taken a good prize, a ship laden with cocoa, in anger and wrath we have hurled overboard this good commodity not regarding the worth and goodness of it, but calling it in bad Spanish *cagaruta de carnero*, or sheep shit in good English.'[3] Chocolate eventually made its British debut, along with tea and coffee, in the mid-seventeenth century. (The first record of coffee drinking was by a Cretan student at Balliol College, Oxford in 1647, and by 1663 there were 82 coffee-houses in London.) The celebrated diarist Samuel Pepys refers to chocolate several times, writing on 3 May 1664, for example, 'Up; and being ready, went by agreement to Mr. Blands and there drank my morning draught in good Chocolatte, and slabbering my band sent home for another.'[4]

By the eighteenth century, much of the political and cultural life of the nobility, gentry and burgeoning middle class in England centred on London's coffee and chocolate houses. Such places were frequented by members of one parliamentary party or another and often became virtual headquarters. One of the oldest was the Cocoa-tree Chocolate House in St James's Street, a well-known meeting place for Jacobites. Another, White's

Chocolate House, was known for its lively politics and high-stakes gambling. (In the mid-eighteenth century, an inner club had developed with access for only approved customers, and it is said that on one wet day Lord Arlington bet £3000 on which of two raindrops would be the first to reach the bottom of a window pane.)

In the rest of Europe, habits of chocolate consumption varied from country to country. In Spain, many cities had guilds of chocolate grinders, and in 1772 there were nearly 150 grinders in Madrid alone. It required six years of apprenticeship to learn the trade, and qualified grinders often went from house to house to serve customers, thereby guarding against adulteration with substances such as almonds, pine nuts, flour, acorns, and bread and cake crumbs. In Italy, chocolate was used imaginatively in cooking, not only in cakes but also in pastries, pastas, and meat dishes. The priest Felici Libera, who was based in Trento in the Alps in the eighteenth century, wrote a cookbook that included an unappetizing recipe for sliced liver that was to be dipped in chocolate, floured, dipped again, then fried. In France, the great innovations were in desserts and sweets, with customers being tempted by chocolate concoctions such as biscuits, pastilles in different shapes, mousses, conserves, marzipans, and creams.

Throughout this period of its history, debate continued about the health properties, or otherwise, of chocolate. Dr Giovanni Batista Felici, physician to the Tuscan court, was a naysayer, warning in 1728 that it shortened life, thickened the blood and caused palpitations, and that in children it awakened 'such an agitation that in no way can they be quiet or sit in one place'.[5] In contrast, an admirably wide-ranging argument for chocolate was advanced by the politician, lawyer and gastronome Jean Anthelme Brillat-Savarin (1755–1826), who recommended it for 'all those who have to work while they might be sleeping, men of wit who feel temporarily deprived of their intellectual powers, those who find the weather oppressive, time dragging, the atmosphere depressing'.[6] It was widely believed to be an aphrodisiac and often features in the correspondence of the infamous Marquis de Sade, who would request it from his long-suffering wife when he was in prison.

The eighteenth century saw a rapid rise in consumerism, with ever-burgeoning numbers of small manufacturers turning out vast quantities of goods. In England, the Industrial Revolution inevitably affected the way chocolate was produced. Walter Churchman was the first chocolate manufacturer in Britain, with premises in Bristol. He had been granted a patent for a water engine by George II, which he used to grind the beans more finely than was possible by hand. In 1731, *Farley's Bristol Newspaper* enthused that the superior smoothness thus obtained meant that the resulting chocolate would be 'less offensive to weak digestions, being by this method made free of grit and gross particles'.[7]

It is at this point that the Quakers enter the story. First the Frys in Bristol and later the Rowntrees in York and the Cadburys in Birmingham. The histories of the three firms are intertwined. Sometimes they conferred on spiritual matters; sometimes they were in direct competition; and occasionally the atmosphere soured. In the next chapter, we'll trace the histories of the three firms in turn.

Chapter 2

Quaker chocolate firms: Fry, Cadbury, and Rowntree

Joseph Fry (1728–1787) had impeccable Quaker family credentials: his ancestors had entertained George Fox, one of the main founders of Quakerism, in their house in Wiltshire, and in 1684 Zephania Fry's faith had landed him in prison. Joseph had trained as an apothecary and he moved to Bristol when he was about 20, opening a small shop in 1753. It was a period in which apothecary windows commonly displayed leeches, but Joseph had learnt about the properties of plants and herbs during his training and was familiar with theories about the benefits of chocolate. In about 1756 he began to sell cocoa in the form of oily flakes and powder suspended in a liquid. It sounds unappetizing, but Joseph successfully promoted it as a nutritious health drink.

Bristol was home to Walter Churchman's chocolate factory, recall, now being run by his son Charles, with its patented machine for producing smooth cocoa. When Charles died in 1761, Joseph, along with his business partner, John Vaughan, was able to buy both the chocolate business and the patent. The new Churchman's Chocolate was much superior to Fry's original recipe, and although heavy import duties meant that the chocolate cure was expensive (in 1771, a pound of Fry's vanilla chocolate cost a week's agricultural wage), the business thrived. In fact, Joseph was something of an entrepreneur. Alongside chocolate, he was involved in soap-boiling, candle-making, the manufacture of china, and, notably, type-founding: in 1758, along with his partner, William Pyne, he cut a fount of Greek types for Oxford University.

When Joseph died, the business was taken over by his widow, Anna, and son Joseph Storrs Fry I (1767–1835). In 1795, the latter installed one of the first steam engines in Britain, a huge clanking contraption that generated press interest across the country and was regarded by his astonished employees as one of the 'wonders of the world', and he was also granted a patent for a new machine to roast beans. Joseph Storrs brought his three sons—Joseph II, Francis, and Richard—on board in 1822, adopting the name J. S. Fry & Sons. By 1824, when the Cadburys were just approaching the starting block, the Frys were using 40 per cent of the cacoa imported into Britain. In 1835 the business passed to the brothers, who produced a cheap Pearl Cocoa, which contained arrowroot to absorb some of the cacoa fat, and a more expensive finely ground Soluble Cocoa. A significant moment came in 1847, when they experimented with mixing their cocoa powder with its by-product, the excess cacoa fat. The result was a rich creamy paste that could be pressed into a mould and left to set. It was the first solid chocolate bar available in Britain. Chocolate had been transformed from a drink to a portable, affordable snack, although solid chocolate would not overtake drinking chocolate as the main industry product until 1919. The chocolate-coated Cream Stick followed in 1866, and, in 1873, the world's first chocolate Easter egg.

Francis took a key role in running the business, but outside work he was a strong advocate for the abolition of slavery and a leading authority on bibles. By the time of his death in 1886, his collection ran to 1300 and was one of the finest in the world. He would studiously compare up to 40 bibles at a time, noting discrepancies, and he produced a facsimile of the only known copy of Tyndale's first edition of the New Testament, printed in 1525/26.

The serious-mindedness evident in Francis' biblical studies is apparent in the way he ran the firm. The rules that were in force in 1851 would have left his employees in no doubt that frivolity would not be tolerated in the workplace. They included '(5) All Day and Piece workers are expected to attend the scripture teaching at a quarter to 9 a.m. As soon as the bell rings for reading, every person to go immediately into the room and the Timekeeper to bolt the door five minutes after the bell has rung. (6) No person to use or eat any cocoa or chocolate... (7) No person to sing or make noises on the premises'.[1]

In 1878, Francis' nephew Joseph Storrs Fry II (the son of Joseph II) took over the reins as chair. Joseph Storrs II had many good qualities: he made numerous charitable donations and held the important Quaker role of clerk of Yearly Meeting for 13 years.[2] He lacked, however, any wider interests: art, science, nature, and social intercourse all failed to engage him. Furthermore, he was introverted, shy, and living with his mother when he took over the company at age 52. His lack of vision might have been behind Fry's decision to keep production in the centre of Bristol at a time when, as we will see, the Rowntrees and Cadburys were building new factories in the country. Descriptions of the Fry factory setup have a touch of Heath Robinson about them: the packing department was housed in an old Baptist chapel, and the church of St Bartholomew became part of the factory complex. Furthermore, Fry refused to advertise: along with many Quakers, they viewed exaggerated claims with disdain and believed that quality would speak for itself.

The conservatism of Joseph Storrs Fry II, an inefficient factory system, a reluctance to advertise, and increased competition from Cadbury and Rowntree meant that Fry's profits gradually fell, and in 1919 they merged with Cadbury to form the British Cocoa and Chocolate Company. By this time, Cadbury had assets worth three times those of Fry, so had the controlling interest. When Bertie Cadbury accepted an offer from the Frys to start work in Bristol, he found the manufacturing process to be shambolic: there were 24 factories, with partially manufactured goods being transported by horse-drawn boxcart through narrow, congested roads; goods were disappearing from doors that opened onto the street; and two of the directors were barely on speaking terms. The board of the new company soon decided to abandon the hotchpotch of Bristol factories and build a new one in the country. Thus in 1920, Bertie and the Fry directors walked along the railway lines leaving Bristol until they found a suitable site, bounded by the River Avon and the main Bristol-to-London railway. The factory was duly built and named Somerdale. The merger is a good place to leave Bristol for Birmingham, to see how Cadbury rose from being the new kid on the block when Fry was at its peak to becoming the dominant partner.

The Cadbury story starts with Richard Tapper Cadbury, who in 1794 bought a draper's shop in Birmingham. His son John was apprenticed to a Quaker tea dealer in Leeds when he was 15, and seven years later began working in a teahouse in London. While there, he recognised the potential of a new exotic commodity — the cacao bean. In 1824, John returned to Birmingham and set up a tea and coffee shop next to the draper's, now being run by his brother Benjamin. He advertised his business in the local paper, drawing attention to cocoa nibs as 'affording a most nutritious beverage for breakfast'.[3]

John clearly had a flair for shopkeeping, installing a stunning window of small plates of glass in a mahogany frame that was such a novelty it drew people from miles around. Inside, he displayed his exotic wares amongst blue Chinese vases, Asian figurines, and ornamental tea chests, and even employed a Chinese worker in Oriental dress. Initially, John ground cacao beans in the back of the shop with a pestle and mortar, and the rich aroma of ground cacao, coffee and loose tea must have enticed customers in from the street. By 1847, however, he had set up a small cocoa works on Bridge Street. The reporter Walter White visited the site and wrote of a storehouse crammed with cacao beans from the Caribbean, a roasting chamber that was home to a 20-horse steam engine that blazed with heat and noise, and a room with shafts, wheels and straps on strange-looking machines. By 1861, however, John was grieving for the death of his wife, Candia, and taking long trips searching for a cure for his rheumatoid arthritis. The business was struggling, and his sons Richard and George, both in their early twenties, were called in to help.

Richard was jovial, relaxed, and usually smiling. He was planning to marry, enjoyed painting and sports, and would have been happy just to make a living out of the chocolate business. George, however, was driven and ambitious. 'He was not a man but a purpose', wrote his biographer.[4] The brothers faced some difficult decisions. Bankruptcy in Quaker circles would have brought great shame and possible expulsion from the Society, as falling into debt was considered a form of theft. They decided to invest the £4000 they had each inherited from their mother in the business, worked long hours, and cut all unnecessary expenses. Richard concentrated on sales, and George on purchasing, policy, and development. George was eager to learn from people who had succeeded and approached the Frys for advice. Francis' son, Francis James, was very obliging and took him to meet other chocolate manufacturers: Fry's sales were approaching £100,000 a year, so they clearly did not see the Cadburys as competition. Despite the brothers' best efforts, however, within four years nearly all of Richard's inheritance had gone, and George had only £1500. Richard was contemplating becoming a surveyor, and George was thinking of taking up tea-planting in the Himalayas.

What turned things round was George's realisation that the key to success was refined cocoa. Cocoa at the time was fatty (from the fat in the bean), and cocoa manufacturers added a host of unsavoury, and occasionally poisonous, additives ranging from brick dust to veal fat to make the powder soluble and drinkable. In Holland, a cocoa firm run by Coenraad van Houten had mechanized the separation of the fat from the cacao bean, decreasing the fat content of cocoa from over 50 per cent to less than 30 per cent, thereby reducing or even eliminating the need for additives. George went to Holland, risked most of his remaining inheritance on one of van Houten's machines, and the 10-ft cast iron contraption duly arrived by canal. Although the resulting product was pure it was expensive, and sales were poor. So, in a last-ditch attempt to save the business, the Cadburys sought endorsements from the medical profession for the purity and health benefits of their product and, bucking the traditional Quaker disdain for advertising, put up posters in shops and advertised on London buses. Richard came up with the heartfelt if not exactly catchy slogan, 'Absolutely Pure, Therefore Best'. Soon, the Cadbury name was synonymous with purity, and sales grew. Furthermore, now that they had an excess of cocoa butter from using the press, the brothers experimented with eating chocolate and launched the Fancy Box of chocolates. In a curious departure from the traditional Quaker preference for plainness, the boxes were extravagantly decorated with satin and lace and could be used for storage long after the chocolates had been eaten. Some were adorned with Richard's paintings: in 1869, the *Birmingham Gazette* enthused about a picture of a 'blue eyed maiden some six summers old, neatly dressed in a muslin frock, trimmed with lace, nursing a cat'.[5] The model in this case was Richard's daughter Jessie and her favourite kitten.

Figure 2: Advert depicting a scientist producing 'pure' Cadbury's cocoa in about 1890 (public domain)

As the business finally began to thrive, the premises at Bridge Street were becoming increasingly cramped. (One employee remembered leaving chocolates on the windowsill to cool and then losing the entire morning's work when someone accidentally knocked them into the yard below.) Crucially, when it came to deciding where and how to expand, the brothers were informed by the knowledge they had gained in the Adult Schools movement (of which more in the next chapter) about the squalid living conditions endured by many and the conditions in other factories. 'We consider that our people spend the greater part of their lives at their work,' they declared, 'and we wish to make it less irksome by environing them with pleasant and wholesome sights, sounds and conditions.'[6] In 1878 they settled on a site near Selly Oak, which had excellent transport links, being bordered by a canal and close to a railway. The site was cut through by a trout stream known as the Bourn, and, in a nod to the acknowledged quality of French chocolate, they named it Bournville.

The new factory was spacious and light but had no south-facing windows in order to prevent the chocolate from overheating, and it was all on one level, so that goods did not have to be carried upstairs. There was a kitchen, a heated cloakroom to dry wet clothes, a large field for men's sports, a garden with swings for the girls (most of whom started work at 14), orchards with plum, pear and cherry trees, and 16 cottages for key staff.

The business grew, and by the early 1900s there were over 4000 employees. Care for staff, which in the early days was achieved through personal knowledge of problems, became more structured. Dr H. Richardson was appointed as the first resident medical officer in 1902, and he was later joined by a female doctor and four trained nurses with massage certificates, who visited employees at home and acted like today's district nurses. Women recovering from serious illness could go to the firm's own convalescence house—the beautiful Froome Bank in Herefordshire—where they stayed for a minimum of three weeks. A dentist was employed in 1905, which must have been a huge relief to many, as 98 of every 100 starters were found to be suffering from toothache. Efforts were also made to improve the lives of individual employees, which, of course, benefitted not just the employee but the business. Edward Cadbury (George's son) recorded all these interventions. A typical example reads: 'Beatrice, a card box learner, was industrious but her work was poor. Her shoulders were very round, and she walked badly. She said when interviewed that she was very fond of books and liked figures. She was given several months' leave of absence, during which she attended the Works gymnastics classes, and she greatly improved in health and general appearance. She was then transferred to the Wages Department, having done well in classes in Mathematics.'[7]

At the turn of the century, the elusive prize for British chocolatiers was the production of a good-quality milk chocolate bar. It was a major technical challenge, as the milk lost its flavour when heated or became lumpy when mixed with chocolate ingredients, or the resulting chocolate turned rancid. The Swiss Daniel Peter was the first to crack the process, in 1886, after years of experiments. The British loved it. In America, Milton Hershey also succeeded. Accounts of his eureka moment vary, but the cynical version, denied by the company, says Hershey made use of a large batch of slightly soured milk powder shipped from Europe, with the resulting chocolate selling well. Rowntree and Fry also had milk chocolate products, although they were inferior to those manufactured by the Swiss. At Cadbury, the task fell to George's 26-year-old son George Jr, who was joined by a chemist, engineer, confectioner, and foreman. Apparently, he was so obsessed with the challenge that one night he woke up delirious and trundled his young wife, Edith, round the bedroom, thinking she was a milk churn. Success finally came in 1904, and launch was set for 1905. The bar was originally to be called Dairy Maid, but when a Cadbury's salesman called at a confectionary shop in Plymouth and couldn't resist boasting of the upcoming launch, the owner's daughter declared that Dairy Milk would be a 'much daintier' name. It soon became the clear favourite among British brands, and in 1910 Cadbury's sales inched for the first time past those of Fry.

This product development was taking place at a particularly distressing time for the Cadburys and, to a lesser extent, for other chocolatiers. Briefly, in the early 1900s, Richard's son William became aware that slaves were being used on cacao plantations on the islands of Sao Tomé and Principe in the Gulf of Guinea: the Portuguese were effectively forcing men and women to sign 'voluntary' labour contracts in their territory of Angola and shipping them to the plantations. William travelled to Lisbon to investigate, and on his return discussed the matter with the Frys and Rowntrees. Portuguese ministers assured him that the situation would improve, but it was decided to send an investigator, Joseph Burtt, to the islands to gather information. When he returned in 1907, Burtt confirmed that workers were held in 'practical slavery', their services having been procured by 'cruel and villainous methods'. Working conditions were horrendous. The Quakers approached the British government, who pleaded for more time in order to avoid antagonizing the Portuguese. After much discussion, Cadbury decided to keep buying the cacao, in the hope that this would give them some leverage in improving conditions. But in 1908, matters were brought to a head when the *Standard* broke the story, claiming that Cadbury was benefiting from slavery and pointing the finger at George Sr in particular. The white hands of the Bournville chocolate makers with their daily prayers, stormed the paper, are 'helped by black and brown hands, toiling in plantations, or hauling loads through swamp and forest'.[8] Cadbury sued the paper for libel, and the resulting court case attracted a huge amount of attention. William was calm and composed in the stand, explaining the firm's reasoning, but George, now in his seventies, found it harder and there were cries of 'Shame!' The ruling went in Cadbury's favour, although the settlement of just one farthing hinted that the jurors were not satisfied with the way Cadbury had acted. The publicity that was generated in England and America, however, meant that the Portuguese government amended their practice of bonded labour, and according to one account 14,000 slave-workers were repatriated.

As we saw above, Cadbury merged with Fry in 1919, and in the 1920s they launched the Flake, Creme Egg, and Fruit and Nut Bar. Barrow Cadbury, Richard's son, was at the helm, and William's signature was adapted to create the now well-known logo. The Bournville factory was revamped in the early 1930s, when over a mile of conveyor belts was installed, and by the end of the decade it was churning out a million bars of Dairy Milk a day. Chocolate was no longer the food of the gods but a routine purchase. Inevitably, World War II slowed down growth. Ingredients were hard to obtain, and in 1941 Dairy Milk was replaced with the much inferior Ration chocolate. The Bournville chocolate factory was covered in green netting, and the Moulding Department turned out not chocolate bars but gun doors for Spitfires.

Commercial television launched in 1955, and Cadbury was on air the very first evening with an advertisement for drinking chocolate. As Rowntree launched their own successful campaigns ('Have a break—Have a Kit Kat'), Cadbury countered with beautiful women seductively eating Flakes and a dashing man in black heroically delivering chocolates, 'all because the lady loves Milk Tray'.

In 1962, amidst concern that many Fry and Cadbury family members had capital tied up in the business and no open market for their shares, the decision was made to go public. The inevitable result was that the board now had to report to independent shareholders who demanded profit. In 1965, Adrian Cadbury, a member of the fourth generation, became chair, and agreed to a merger with Schweppes, realising that the two companies combined would have greater resources for research and development: in 1969, he became joint managing director and deputy chairman of Cadbury Schweppes. Internationally, the company expanded its operations to India, a move that necessitated establishing a dairy herd for a milk supply (cattle that were used to the heat of Rajasthan were inseminated with imported Ayrshire semen), and later pushed into Russia in the wake of the collapse of the Soviet Union. At home, their market share waxed (e.g., with the launch of Cadbury's Wispa in 1983) and waned (e.g., with the launch of Rowntree's Yorkie bar in 1976). Dominic Cadbury (Adrian's brother) was the final Cadbury chairman: when he retired in 2000, the firm was without a family member on the board for the first time.

Cadbury and Schweppes de-merged in 2008, the total value of the two companies now being worth more separately than the combined value. Then, in 2009, Cadbury's chair, Roger Carr, was approached by Irene Rosenfeld, chair of the American food giant Kraft Foods, about a takeover. In early 2010, after a turbulent few months, Kraft finally offered a price that was acceptable to shareholders. British consumers were angry, fearing that production would be moved abroad. Campaigns were launched to save the Curly Wurly. And Adrian and Dominic described the takeover simply as 'a tragedy'.

The third Quaker family chocolate dynasty started with Joseph Rowntree Sr, whose father owned a grocer's in Scarborough. On his twenty-first birthday, having clattered his way to York on the outside of a coach, his head full, no doubt, of ambitious dreams, Joseph and his friend James Backhouse attended an auction at the Elephant and Castle in Skeldergate. The auctioneer was drunk, but on James' suggestion the young men dunked his head in a bucket of cold water to sober him up. Thus in 1822 Joseph Sr became the owner of a shop at 28 Pavement, York. It was in a prime location next to various markets and fairs, and the business thrived.

When Joseph Sr died in 1859, the grocer's business passed to two of his sons, John (25) and Joseph (23). The youngest son, Henry Isaac, who did not share his brothers' or father's business acumen, had joined Tuke and Company, eventually becoming manager of the cocoa, chocolate and chicory department. Tuke's had, unusually, been started by a woman. Mary Tuke was a Quaker, the daughter of a blacksmith, although she was orphaned when young. Unmarried at 30, she decided to go into business as a grocer, and when she died in 1752 she left the business to her nephew William Tuke. (William is also remembered for founding The Retreat in York, an institution that established a revolutionary regime of kindness to the mentally ill.) Thereafter, the business passed from father to son and became more specialized, focusing on tea dealing and on chocolate and cocoa manufacture. No sons were interested in the business when Samuel Tuke died in 1857, and in 1862 the company was split. Henry bought the chocolate and cocoa division with money left to him by his father (an inheritance of £1000 and a sum of £2000 administered by John and Joseph, presumably in lieu of a partnership at Pavement).

The business was based in Castlegate, but Henry relocated, having purchased a motley collection of buildings, including an iron foundry, several dilapidated cottages and a tavern, bounded on one side by the foul-smelling River Ouse and on the other by a street called Tanner's Moat. The main product was Tuke's Superior Rock Cocoa, which Henry gleefully relabelled 'Rowntree's Prize Medal Rock Cocoa' after it won one of 133 medals at a Yorkshire Exhibition. Light-hearted and with a good sense of humour, he liked to quote Deuteronomy: 'For their Rock is not as our Rock, even our enemies themselves being judges.'

The factory setup was far from ideal, however. There was a workshy donkey who should have transported goods but preferred taking a Turkish bath at the steam pipe that Henry had rigged up in the stable, and a distracting parrot in the girls' workroom that Henry had trained to screech, 'Now lasses, get on with your work!' The accounting system was somewhat short on rigour: the foreman, Hanks, paid everyone out of a hat filled with silver and copper, trustingly asking each employee 'How much time has thee got?' Henry himself could often be seen up to the elbows in vats of oily cocoa and loved trying out ad hoc adaptations to the machinery the minute he had an idea for improvement. Furthermore, from 1868 he diverted time, money, and staff to producing a weekly paper, *The Yorkshire Express*.

Perhaps not surprisingly, bankruptcy loomed, and in 1869 Joseph withdrew the money he had invested in the Pavement grocer's in an attempt to help his brother. Although he tightened up the way the works was run, the Rowntrees could not or would not buy a van Houten press, so there was a limit on the quality of their products. Joseph also refused to boost sales by advertising, dismissing it as 'puffery'. The practice at the time was for shopkeepers to use their own branding on products, and when one shopkeeper made extravagant claims about the quality of cocoa supplied by Rowntree, Joseph was not slow to express his disapproval: 'It is *not* a pure ground cocoa. It is *not* produced from the finest Trinidad Nuts. It is *not* the "best for family use". In fact, the whole thing is a sham, not very creditable to anyone concerned with it.'[9] The firm struggled throughout the 1870s making only small profits, and in some years a loss.

Success came when Joseph took on a French confectioner named Claude Gaget, who in 1879 had called claiming to have come up with his own version of a fruity, chewy pastille. It was 1881 before Joseph was satisfied with Gaget's sweet, but the wait was worth it. The pastilles helped to turn the business around, and Joseph was finally able to buy a van Houten press, many years after the Cadburys had used one to transform the quality of their products. One notable hiccup in the trajectory of success, however, was Joseph's attempt to understand the 'Dutching' process, a procedure developed by Coenraad van Houten (of press fame) that involved adding alkaline salts to the bean, which made the cocoa less bitter. The process was a closely guarded secret, but in 1885 Joseph hired the Dutchman Cornelius Hollander, who claimed to understand it. Hollander insisted in working in private, kept his workroom padlocked, and aggravated colleagues with unreasonable requests, but no results were forthcoming. Eventually, staff broke into the room only to discover that Hollander knew next to nothing about the process, and a subsequent police raid on his house revealed that he had stolen equipment and made drawings of machines.

Henry had died from complications following an appendicitis in 1883, but over the coming years the next generation joined the firm: Joseph's sons John Wilhelm and Seebohm, Henry's son Frank, and John's son Arnold. Significant changes followed. Joseph shared the Cadbury brothers' view that it would be easier to improve conditions for staff out of town. Thus, in 1890 he bought a site on Haxby Road on the outskirts of York, with John Wilhelm becoming heavily involved in the relocation plans. Furthermore, Joseph's reluctance to advertise was overcome, and here it was Arnold who rose to the challenge, relishing the creative freedom the role offered. Elect Cocoa had been launched in 1887—a light powder that could be sold without added sugar or arrowroot—and Arnold's first stunt, in the mid-1890s, was to buy a car and install a gigantic replica tin of Elect Cocoa behind the driver. Cars were a novelty, and as it toured the north of the country at a leisurely pace it drew crowds and made headlines (especially when it caused chaos by breaking down in Sheffield). Then, in 1897, he covered a barge with adverts for Elect Cocoa and had it pulled down the Thames by two mechanically propelled swans before the bemused crowds that had gathered to watch the boat race. Seebohm, for his part, had read chemistry at Owens College in Manchester and created a laboratory to help with new product lines.

Seebohm took over as chair in 1923, and Joseph died in 1925. Cadbury at this time was launching Flake, Fruit and Nut, and Crunchie, and Rowntree had no answer until the 1930s, when George Harris, who had married into the Rowntree family, came up with a tempting array of popular new products, including the Kit Kat (1935), Dairy Box (1936), Smarties (1937), and Polo (1939). The 1930s was also a period in which the relationship between Rowntree and Cadbury deteriorated. Rowntree had developed the Aero and was seeking a patent for its production process. Cadbury mounted a legal challenge, arguing that some of the processes involved were already in use at Bournville. They were perhaps irked by Rowntree's advertising strategy for Aero, which implicitly targeted Dairy Milk in the claim that Aero 'digests twice as fast as old-fashioned milk chocolate'. In the past, such differences would have been resolved by the Society of Friends, but by this time the Quaker presence on the boards had diminished. The outbreak of war, however, caused the two firms to put their differences aside.

The Quaker involvement in Rowntree finally came to an end in 1988, when the Swiss-German firm Jacob Suchard and Nestlé entered a bidding war. Both bids faced opposition from those wanting to keep Rowntree British, and Nestlé's bid was greeted with additional outrage because the firm was being boycotted over the marketing of infant formula as an alternative to breast-feeding in developing countries where mothers did not have access to clean water. Dominic Cadbury argued that the solution was for Cadbury to take over Rowntree, pointing out that competition was not an issue if you looked at global rather than national market share, but he was told that if he proceeded he would be referred to the Monopolies Commission. In mid-

June, Nestlé raised its bid to £2.5 billion, and the Rowntree shareholders voted to accept.

The histories of these three Quaker firms reveal some common themes. In true Quaker fashion, those in the first generation were successful shopkeepers. The second generations, of Richard and George Cadbury and Joseph Rowntree, made successes out of struggling fledgling family chocolate concerns partly because of the stigma attached to bankruptcy in Quaker circles. And all three firms benefited from the Quaker network. Francis James Fry took George Cadbury under his wing as a young man, and Joseph Rowntree Sr took on Quaker apprentices. Henry Rowntree wrote to his brother Joseph in 1857 about one of these apprentices: 'We had George Cadbury to dinner and tea ... our new hand, he has not been at all accustomed to the retail trade, and will never, I think, make much out of it, he seems kind and chearful [sic].'[10] We will see just how spectacularly wrong Henry was in the next chapter.

Chapter 3

George Cadbury: 'Not a man but a purpose'

Figure 3: George Cadbury (public domain)

George's life was characterized by the integration of his religious beliefs and spiritual experience into his business. It was something that came naturally, as he grew up in a household where an active, socially aware religion and work were both taken seriously. For the Cadburys, the religious focal points were Sunday and Wednesday mornings, when the family would go to the old meeting house on Bull Street for a Meeting for Worship based around a communal, listening silence. On a Wednesday, this meant that John Cadbury would close his shop for an hour or two, and the children (five boys and a girl) would miss school for the morning. This experiential practice of paying attention to God, who could be found within, was interpreted within a Christian framework, and as a boy George used to carry a Bible in his pocket and memorize passages as he walked.

These spiritual practices and beliefs, which affirm the presence of God in all, are closely linked to the Quaker tradition of fighting against social injustice. If God can be found in all people, then all are worthy of care and respect. (Elizabeth Fry, wife of a cousin of the Bristol Frys, for example, at one point featured on a Bank of England £5 note for her nineteenth-century work in prison reform.) George could not fail to be influenced by his parents, John and Candia, who both embraced this tradition with conviction and passion. John was Overseer of the Poor from 1830 to 1840 (with one of his first actions being to end the committee's habit of meeting for a 'sumptuous repast' before dealing with the matter of paupers), and in the 1840s he chaired the Steam Engine Committee, responsible for tackling the debilitating smoke and smog belching from Birmingham's many chimneys. Both he and Candia were also long-standing supporters of the temperance movement. Gin was cheap and widely available, and it was not uncommon for the children of alcoholics to die of neglect. In the 1850s, John gave talks and enlisted friends to gather data on the number of pubs, licensed victuallers, and drunkards in Birmingham, and Candia visited pubs and pleaded with publicans on behalf of children, a practice she continued even when tuberculosis had confined her to a bathchair.

George's childhood also instilled in him a deep love of outdoor physical exercise and nature, along with a conviction that God could be found in the natural world. The family home was in a leafy district of Edgbaston and had a large garden with peach and nectarine trees. Encouraged by their father, who measured the circumference of the lawn and ascertained that 21 laps equalled one mile, the Cadbury children would regularly run a mile before breakfast with their hoops, or accompany John and the family dogs on his morning walk across nearby fields. As slums gradually encroached on the countryside, George was struck by how people suffered physically, morally, and spiritually without contact with nature.

Although the Cadburys were reasonably well off, their lifestyle was shaped by the Puritan influence within Quakerism, such that self-indulgence and luxury were frowned upon. John had stopped playing the flute in deference to his father's will and did not allow an easy chair into the house until he was 70. The children's reading was largely confined to books such as *Pilgrim's Progress*, and although they had ponies, they were expected to look after them themselves. According to his friend and biographer Alfred Gardiner, this cultural narrowness meant that George was totally focused on the business and the benefits it could bring.

George began to find his own way of living out his faith when at age 20 he started to teach within the Adult School movement. The first school had been set up by the Methodist William Singleton and the Quaker Samuel Fox in Nottingham in the 1790s to educate young women in lace and hosiery factories, and the movement was brought to Birmingham by Quakers in 1845. The schools were non-denominational and aimed to combat illiteracy, partly to enable people to read the Bible for themselves (roughly a fifth of men and a third of women could not read or write). They took place on Sunday mornings, and in the early days the classes were divided into two—half studied reading and writing while the other half studied the Bible, and then they swapped. Some men came from respectable working homes, others were from slums, and still others were recruited from public houses or even at prison gates. All were made to feel welcome, even if they arrived drunk or in rags.

George started by teaching a class of boys, and four years later was given a classroom and assigned the adult Class XIV, an association that would continue for the next half century. Teaching at the school meant that a Sunday 'day of rest' was anything but. George rose at 5.30 a.m., left the house at 6.30 a.m., and covered the five miles to the school initially by horse and later by bike. Every week he provided a box of flowers, with each man choosing his favourite. 'Mr Cadbury's flowers' became well known in the area, and George loved to see children running to discover what flower their father had chosen. He was convinced that children had an instinctive love of flowers and that the love of flowers led to the love of all natural and wholesome things.

About 4000 men passed through Class XIV over the years, and George organized reunions and maintained personal contact with some former students. The school undoubtedly had an effect on these men, but the men also had an effect on George: he once even admitted to admiring housebreakers, as he identified with their enjoyment of risk. More significantly, he concluded that the best way to improve a person's circumstances was to raise their ideals, and that to do this it was necessary to provide better living conditions. How could someone cultivate good ideals when they lived in a slum and the only possible place of recreation was a public house? The material and the spiritual react on each other, he insisted. In later life, George would say that it was his experiences in the Adult School that made the success at Bournville possible, because through the men he encountered he gained a sense of the waste and degradation of life under the modern industrial system.

At the same time as George was devoting Sundays to teaching, he and Richard were trying to turn their father's business around and avoid the shame of bankruptcy. Here the boys' deliberately relatively spartan upbringing proved a great asset. Both had agreed to invest their inheritance and were used to living frugally, but Richard was about to marry, so there was a limit on what he could be expected to sacrifice. George, however, stripped every habit and expense that would distract him from his purpose. He did not smoke or drink anyway, and in addition cut out the morning paper, tea and coffee, and largely stopped playing cricket and boating. He got up at 5.15 a.m. in the summer and 6 a.m. in the winter, went to work, returned home for lunch, then back to work, where he took a tea of bread, butter and water before finally returning home at

9 p.m. in winter and at 6 p.m. in summer (to allow some time for recreation). By living like this he cut his expenses to £25 a year, but even so after 5 years he had only £1500 left and Richard had almost nothing. 'If I had been married there would have been no Bournville today,' he said later. 'It was just the money that I saved by living so sparely that carried us over the crisis.'[1]

One employee, T. J. O'Brien, gives some insight into those early years when the business was struggling, emphasizing both the hands-on approach of the brothers and their relationship with the staff: 'I never knew men work harder than our masters who were indeed more like fathers to us,' he claimed. 'Sometimes they were working in the manufactory, then packing in the warehouse, then again all over the country getting orders.'[2] O'Brien had the hard physical task of beating the crème by hand, and the brothers would often take a stint (although he remembered the severe reprimand he received when one day he left them to it and went home). George thrived on the challenge: 'There is certainly untold pleasure in having to contend with overwhelming difficulties,' he enthused. 'And I sometimes pity those who have never had to go through it. Success is infinitely sweeter after struggle.'[3]

Coupled with this undoubted grit and commitment, George was prepared to take risks. As we saw in the last chapter, when he travelled to Holland to buy the van Houten press the brothers were nearly out of money and the possibility of failure was very real, but George was determined. 'I went off to Holland without knowing a word of Dutch, saw the manufacturer, with whom I had to talk entirely by signs and a dictionary, and bought the machine,' he recalled. 'It was by prompt action such as this that my brother and I made our business.'[4]

By the late 1870s, with the business finally beginning to make a profit, the brothers were able to explore the idea of building a 'factory in a garden'. Inspired by the ideas of John Ruskin, who was pointing to the role of the economy and society in perpetuating poverty, and informed by their experiences in the Adult School, they were questioning why a factory had to be in a slum and wondering how the conditions endured by the poor could be improved. Critics scoffed at the idea that altruism could be applied to business and that fresh air was relevant, predicting that the venture would end in disaster. But in 1878 the rural site later named Bournville had been decided on. It was an exciting time. George would bring his family to the site in the firm's horse-drawn van, and while 6-year-old Edward played in the mud and admired the mountains of bricks, Richard's 11-year-old son William was drawn to the river full of trout. John, by this time in his 80s, slowly wandered the site with a walking stick, soberly dressed in a black top hat and dark coat.

Inevitably there were a few teething problems once production moved to the new factory, but George's and Richard's friendly relationship with the staff carried them through. The first winter was bitterly cold and the heating system erratic, but when nearby pools froze over the owners allowed the workers to skate and slide on them. There were also transport difficulties, as the girls had to walk across fields to get to the train station. Fanny Price remembered how in cold and rainy weather, shelter was provided near the old station lodge, and how 'Mr Richard used to stand outside and blow a whistle to intimate that the train was coming so that the girls could run from their dressing room'.[5] Furthermore, the rush to complete Christmas orders meant that it was decided the girls needed to start work at 6 a.m. Because of the lack of trains at that hour, temporary bedrooms were set up in the recently completed houses on the site and in a makeshift dormitory in one of the factory rooms. Presumably, the sense of excitement that Richard and George shared with the staff made the experience of working long hours very different from what it would be today in a large business out solely to make profit. Certainly one employee, Frances Stanley, reminisced that most seemed to have enjoyed the adventure. Another employee, H. E. Johnson, perhaps looking through slightly rose-tinted spectacles, enthused that Richard and George 'were the centre round which everything moved. It was a kindly duocracy and those who served under it ... have nothing but happy recollections of the early days of Bournville'.[6] By 1880, the move to the factory was paying dividends: Cadbury's sales had risen to nearly half those of Fry and they were beginning to expand into Canada, Australia and New Zealand.

In the midst of all these developments, George maintained religious practices at home and at work. Throughout his life, there were family prayers every morning, attended by all who worked in the house. At work in the early days, George had formed a habit of breakfasting with the workforce and reading aloud a book of general interest, and from this came the idea that if daily worship was good in the family group it would also be good in the work context. Initially, the service took the form of a Bible reading followed by a time of silence for prayer, but George realized that the silence was not helpful for everyone so added a hymn and gave a short address. In 1866, as the business grew, he consulted with Joseph Storrs Fry II on the best way to structure the service and the size of the hall needed. The practice was discontinued in 1870, but the staff put together a petition to ask for its resumption. In a circular responding to the petition, George emphasized the value of silent prayer when all might 'wait on the Lord for themselves'. It is a comment that hints that he wanted the spiritual life of his employees to develop, rather than to indoctrinate them. When production moved to Bournville the services continued, and one visitor, Dean Kitchin, described a service he attended in 1910, which clearly made a deep impression. All the women were dressed in white for work (earning them the nickname of the Cadbury's angels), and 'the short reading, kind words and simple prayer, preceded by a hymn sung by three thousand women's voices, was a revelation of religious purity and simplicity at full force'.[7] The poetically inclined C. L. Edwards appreciated the spiritual egalitarianism that shone through: 'There were quiet lanes, quiet in those times, furnishing hallowed spots by rustic stile or scented hedgerow ... one's mind turns to the morning readings organized within the Works and presided over always by the partners, seeking consistently and persistently to draw us workers into a partnership with them of spiritual values.'[8]

On a personal level during these decades, George had married Mary in 1872, with whom he had six children, but was widowed in 1887 when Mary died from a fever possibly associated with complications after the birth of her sixth child, who had died shortly after birth a month previously. The following year he married Elsie, later Dame Elizabeth Cadbury, with whom he had a further six children. Elsie was a strong woman (later described with words such as 'handsome' and 'formidable') who shared George's commitment to social reform. She taught the wives of George's students but also forged her own path through involvement with organizations such as the National Union of Women Workers and the YWCA.

In many ways, George was living the life of a successful Victorian industrialist, buying a series of large houses and employing servants. Even though Quaker attitudes to the arts had softened, however, George never widened his cultural interests. He once remarked to Gardiner, 'Why should I hang fortunes on my walls while there is so much misery in the world?'[9] Clothes held no appeal either: he always seemed to wear the same grey tweed suit, and for special occasions a silk top hat, blissfully unaware of how out of fashion it was.

By 1895, George was ready to fulfil a long-held dream to turn his garden factory into a garden city, to be named Bournville. He appointed the architect William Harvey, who had been inspired by John Ruskin to promote craftsmanship in architecture.

The houses had stepped gables and timber porches, spacious gardens for growing vegetables, and fruit trees were planted before the new owners moved in. There were also excellent sports and recreation facilities, no doubt inspired by George's love of outdoor sports, including a cricket ground, swimming pool, croquet lawn and swings. The village school was built in 1905, with George taking the battle to limit the class size to 45 rather than the usual 55 to Whitehall.

The village was not restricted to Cadbury employees, however. George's ambition went much further: he wanted to create a model community for people in all types of employment that would become a template to raise the livings standards of the poor elsewhere in Britain. He was undoubtedly successful on some measures: in 1919, studies showed that children aged 6 to 12 years in Bournville grew on average two to three inches taller and were eight pounds heavier than their contemporaries in poorer parts of Birmingham, and infant mortality was roughly halved. More generally, J. B. Priestly visited Bournville in 1933 and described it as 'a small outpost of civilisation, still ringed around with barbarism'[10] (although he criticised the lack of 'frivolous' meeting places).

By 1900, the estate included 500 acres of land with 370 houses and was valued at £172,724 (the Bank of England's inflation calculator gives this as over £17 million in 2023). On 14 December of that year, George gave it away in the creation of the Bournville Village Trust. The deeds of the trust spelled out George's aims, namely, to ameliorate the conditions of the working class and to improve their quality of life through improved housing, gardens, and open spaces. He and the family were well aware of the enormity of the act: 'I have seriously considered how far a man is justified in giving away the heritage of his children,' he said at the founding of the trust, 'and have come to the conclusion that my children will be all the better for being deprived of this money. Great wealth is not to be desired, and in my experience of life it is more a curse than a blessing to the families of those who possess it.'[11]

In addition to his work at the factory and village, George was active in various ventures that aimed to improve the lives of the disadvantaged. He was president of the Anti-Sweating League, which sought to stop the exploitation of workers, for example, and he and his son Edward helped to create the National Old Age Pensions League to push for state support for the elderly. Especially close to his heart was the plight of children, and he was often moved to tears at the sight of those who were in rags and neglected. Wanting to improve the lives of disabled children, he bought Woodlands, a large house in spacious grounds, and converted it to a hospital to be run by Birmingham Cripples' Union. For years he visited the children there every Sunday night, armed with chocolate for all. When he and his family moved to the Manor House in Northfield, he erected a large hall called the Barn for entertaining visitors. It could seat 700 children, and in summer he loved to call in at the almost daily parties. A further project was The Beeches in Bournville, which was an invalid home in winter and a camp used for a two-week holiday for children in the summer. It was not uncommon for the children, who lived in industrial slums, suddenly to be 'unaccountably missing' when it was time for them to go home.

On other societal issues, George campaigned through newspapers. In 1901, he was approached by David Lloyd George, who was seeking a Liberal backer for the *Daily News*. George put up £20,000 to join a partnership to purchase the paper, seeing the advantage of a platform to oppose the Boer War (both he and Elsie were shocked at the way the national press was fuelling the appetite for conflict). Advertisers responded by pulling their business, however, so the other partners wanted out, and George felt he had no option other than to buy the paper. In addition to promoting the anti-war message, he used it to expose various social ills: in 1906, for example, he personally funded an exhibition organized by the paper about the horrors of sweated labour. When the Liberal *Morning Leader* and *Star* came up for sale in 1910, George again wanted to use the press as a platform to promote peace and Liberal reforms, and joined forces with the Rowntree family to buy them. The early days were mired in controversy because the papers published gambling news, which was abhorrent to Quakers. Joseph Storrs Fry's brother, Sir Edward Fry, led the Quaker charge of hypocrisy, and implied that George was going into partnership with the devil to aid the Almighty. The *Star*, as an evening paper, would be unthinkable without racing news, so George ended up taking the pragmatic stance of keeping it. As he explained to his son Laurence, 'I sought to be guided by commonsense, and it was evident that the *Star* with betting news and pleading for social reform and for peace was better than the *Star* with betting and opposing social reform, and stirring up strife with neighbouring nations.'[12]

George never intended to make money out of the papers though, and in 1911 he established the Daily News Trust, in the hope 'that it may be of service in bringing the ethical teaching of Jesus Christ to bear upon National questions, and in promoting National Righteousness; for example, that Arbitration should take the place of War'.[13] In a letter to his sons, he explained that he was convinced that the money spent trying to arouse his fellow countrymen to ameliorate the conditions of the poor, forsaken and downtrodden masses through a great newspaper was far more effective than money given to charities.

George was clearly driven, hard-working, hands-on, and deeply concerned for the plight of the poor who were stymied by the way society and industry were structured. Despite his many family, charitable, and business responsibilities, however, he seems to have had the ability to really 'see' the people he encountered on a day-to-day basis. His biography contains many examples of people who attested to George's attention. There was the young Cadbury employee waiting for a train in the snow: George told her to go home because the weather was bad and provided a note saying her wages should not be docked. There were the two elderly ladies on a walk: George invited them back for tea because the sun was hot and they were tired. There was the gardener's child returning from school: George encouraged him to run home so he could ask his mother if he could attend a Punch and Judy show being put on at Woodlands.

This ability to be present to people might have been fostered by George's personal religious practices. In addition to starting the day with a time of family or work worship, it was his habit to end the day with a walk, during which he could take stock of the day and commune with God. 'There is nothing like a walk in the evening to make one realize the presence of God,' he once mused in a speech at Bournville.[14] Throughout the day, too, he was attentive to God's guidance. Sometimes seeking guidance was a deliberate act: the young employee Edward Thackery proudly recalled being called into George's office on several occasions so that they could kneel together in prayer over some weighty business matter. Sometimes this guidance was unsought: he told his biographer that one morning when out riding, 'it was strongly impressed upon my mind that the house and gardens of Woodbrooke should be handed over to the Society of Friends as a college for men and women' (on which more in Chapter 6).[15] Sometimes it took the form of a long-term conviction that required saying 'no' to other opportunities. When the leader of the Liberal party W. E. Gladstone asked George to adopt a parliamentary career in 1892, he replied, 'I belong to the Society of Friends, a body which professes to believe that divine guidance is vouchsafed to those who have faith to ask for it, and so far I have felt I can be of most service to my fellow men in connexion with religious work, and by taking part in social questions.'[16]

As far as his beliefs were concerned, George was convinced that prayer was effective in making things happen. According to his granddaughter Eleanor Wharton, one of his sayings was, 'That, my dear, is the result of my prayer', adding that she believed it was this to which he would attribute his great achievements in the world of business.[17] He was not, however, overly concerned with doctrine, theology, or rituals, and wrote despairingly of the preoccupation of churches with questions of outward observance rather than social issues. What mattered was hastening the time when the spirit of Jesus' sermon on the Mount would prevail. He was convinced that actions were more important than creeds: 'I do not ask a man what he believes,' he once said. 'If he is a drunkard let him put away the drink ... if he is domestic tyrant let him govern his temper. This is the living test.'[18]

George died on 24 October 1922, fittingly just as the Bournville bell rang to signal the end of the working day. Elsie told her friends that 'it was the going home of a conqueror'.[19]

Chapter 4

Joseph Rowntree: Social investigator

Figure 4: Joseph Rowntree (public domain)

Until Joseph was nine, the Rowntree family lived above Joseph Sr's grocery shop at 28 Pavement, York. Outside, market crowds bustled, geese honked on their walk in from the countryside, and the rowdy fairs on Whitsuntide and Martinmas hosted dog fights and fortune tellers. Inside, the family had an almost commune-style living arrangement, sharing their home with up to 12 apprentices—young lads from 13 upwards who had come to learn the grocery trade. A memo from Joseph Sr in 1852 details a set of rules for these apprentices. They sound severe but were probably meant to reassure the families who sent their sons to learn a trade. There were curfews and a firm warning that Pavement was not a suitable place for 'the indolent and the wayward'. There was, however, a clear concern for the social and spiritual development of the boys. Although advising that twenty minutes was sufficient for meals, which had to be taken in shifts, Joseph Sr recognised that meals should be social occasions and therefore clarified that 'it is *not* designed to determine their exact duration'. He concluded with an expression of his 'earnest desire' that 'the household may in all respects maintain those habits and practices in regard to dress, language, etc., which distinguish the religious Society of Friends'.[1] In addition to the apprentices, the Rowntrees often hosted visiting Quakers, especially during Quarterly Meetings in York, when 30 people would eat in shifts and the children would sleep on mattresses on the floor.

The Rowntree children (John, Joseph, Henry, Hannah, and Sarah Jane) attended family prayers every morning and had to learn a Bible verse every day, but despite this regime and the rules set out for the apprentices, they enjoyed a relaxed style of parenting. 'We had the reputation of being very wild children,' Joseph wrote. 'I think that a stranger, coming into the family, would probably have been startled by the freedom we boys enjoyed.'[2] They were educated at home initially, and, much to the governess's consternation, often amused themselves with messy experiments with gas, plaster of Paris and gelatine in the living room, and a favourite game was to see how far down the stairs they could kick the apprentices' beaver hats. Books were abundant, however, and dinner discussions ranged from Macaulay's essays to parliamentary reports. When he was 11, Joseph followed his older brother to the Quaker Bootham school. The head at the time was the visionary John Ford, whose pioneering initiatives in teaching science and extracurricular emphasis on natural history meant that Bootham became known as a nursery for Quaker botanists.

As in the Cadbury household, the Quaker involvement with social issues was prominent. Joseph Sr was concerned about education: he ascertained how many children did not attend school by knocking on doors, and in 1843 helped to modernize the curriculum of Ackworth School. He also set up the York Soup Kitchen in a local tavern and was involved in York County Hospital and a scheme to rehabilitate prostitutes. For young Joseph, a defining experience occurred when his father and

John Ford took him and his older brother John to Ireland during the potato famine. The boys were told to take their botanical notebooks, but it seems likely that one of the purposes of the trip was to gather information for a Quaker relief effort. Joseph was 14 at the time and witnessed exhausted women sitting by the roadside clutching dead babies, and places where the dead had been laid in trenches by those too weak to do more. It was a stark and brutal picture of the effects of poverty, and one that he never forgot.

Running a grocer's in the nineteenth century required a range of skills. There were handwritten accounts to balance, tea and coffee to blend, and goods to price according to quality. Customers depended on the judgement of their local grocer, and grocers branded their own goods as a guarantee of satisfaction. Joseph had started as an apprentice at the Pavement shop after school, and in 1857 went to London to gain experience by working for a large wholesale grocer. He was clearly a serious and conscientious young man and kept his father up to date in detailed letters: 'During the morning brokers are frequently bringing in samples of tea, which I liquor against those we have in stock. In the same way I roast, grind, liquor and taste the samples of coffee. The roasting, to do it perfectly, is a very delicate operation, and I am glad to take every opportunity of increasing my skill. I frequently accompany one of the clerks to the Customs and Docks and also to the Banks. I am gradually getting to understand the system of book-keeping.'[3] When not working, Joseph, spurning light entertainment, visited the House of Commons. He was not impressed with Disraeli, complaining that 'His utterance is hesitating—his argument not very clear—his brilliance seems only to display itself in satire— his arguments seem saturated with party feeling'.[4] Joseph Sr wanted Joseph back in York, however, and after a gentle hint in a letter delivered by his older brother, Joseph returned and was made a partner in the shop in 1857 at age 21.

Joseph quickly settled into life as a respected grocer in York. He started to teach at the Adult School, a weekly Sunday commitment he maintained until he was nearly 60. Again, it was a responsibility he took very seriously, putting a good deal of effort into preparing a weekly 'bright and practical address', a task that he admitted to finding onerous at times. Sometimes he taught men in their own homes, gaining a valuable insight into the living conditions of the poor. He wrote that the opportunity to meet with men who were trying to improve themselves every week was a great blessing and that the experience brought him 'face to face with many of the facts of life'.[5]

When Joseph Sr died in 1859, John (25) and Joseph (23) took over the shop and their father's charitable concerns, with Joseph taking his father's place on the management committee of two Quaker schools. In August 1862 he married Julia Seebohm, a Quaker of German extraction who was well known to the Rowntree family from her time at school in York. The couple had a daughter Julia (known as Lilley) in May of the following year, but the birth weakened Julia and she died that September, probably from meningitis. Joseph's sister Hannah moved in to take care of Lilley, proving to be a devoted aunt. Joseph would marry Julia's cousin, Antoinette Seebohm (known as Tonie), in 1867, but in the years following Julia's death he spent long evenings in the counting-house behind the shop rather than going home.

At this difficult time, he seems to have found solace in investigating the extent of poverty. For more than two generations, people had been moving from the country to the city, and the cholera epidemics of 1848–1849 and 1854 had exposed the horrors of drinking water brown with sewage, of single rooms for a family of 12, and of gin shops that catered for children as young as five. A social conscience was awakening throughout the country, and statistics were beginning to be used to describe social problems. Joseph approached the issue of poverty carefully and methodically, slowly gathering a wide range of statistics for analysis. He prepared tables of the number of illiterate men and women, for example, gleaning his figures from marriage registers, which showed how many could sign their name and how many simply made a 'mark'. His research convinced him that too much of the country's wealth was being spent on armaments and not enough on education, and that there was a connection between poverty, illiteracy and crime.

The result of these hours of solitude spent thinking and poring over numbers was an essay titled 'British Civilization. In what it consists and in what it does *not* consist'. The intention was that it would be read at a conference of Adult School teachers. Joseph did read portions of it, in Bristol and Leeds in 1864, but Joseph Storrs Fry, who was arranging the Bristol conference, asked him to tone down the language, which he felt was 'a little too strong in places'. The following year, he wrote a further essay, 'Pauperism in England and Wales'. Again, he did not hold back, denouncing the Church for not speaking out against atrocities when its own interests were at stake. Commenting on the fact that one-fifth of the population did not have sufficient food and clothing, he concluded that 'It is a monstrous thing that in this land, rich in natural wealth and now rich beyond all precedent, millions of its inhabitants, made in the image of their Creator, should spend their days in a struggle for existence so severe as to blight (where it does not destroy) the higher parts of their nature'.[6]

Joseph might have remained a grocer and social investigator all his life, had it not been for the wild card that was Henry Isaac Rowntree. Henry was clearly cut from a very different cloth than his father and brothers. He was just about bottom in just about every subject at Bootham, and tutoring in reading and a change of school did little to help. He was, however, intelligent, charismatic, creative, funny, and warm-hearted. He threw himself into social events at the Adult School, providing entertainment at the annual tea with magic lanterns and chemistry experiments, and once took 90 working men to Paris for a week. Also active in the York Temperance Society, he organized addresses, recitations and singing at well-attended meetings. His realistic slides of the human stomach with and without alcohol were, it was said, remembered long after the event.

Letters from Joseph Sr reveal an affection and concern for his youngest son, so it was presumably a cool assessment of his lack of ability rather than rejection that was behind his decision not to take Henry on as a partner alongside his older brothers. Instead, as we saw in Chapter 2, Henry bought the Tuke cocoa business and moved production to Tanner's Moat. But what with his other interests and sloppy accounting, not to mention the nagging parrot and spa-loving donkey, bankruptcy was looming, and Joseph stepped in.

It was a huge change. Joseph's whole life as a boy and man had revolved round the Pavement shop, and it had been his refuge when Julia died. Even 20 years later, his early resentment comes across in a letter to Henry's widow. He describes the cocoa business as 'hopelessly embarrassed [with] the bookkeeping in a state of confusion',[7] and goes on to complain of the struggle of learning a new business at 33 and the need to plough nearly his entire fortune into a venture whose owner demonstrated a 'singular inaptitude in business' and who still wanted to publish a paper every Saturday. (He did on another occasion, however, admit that Henry's power of rescuing a drunkard was a far higher power than the power of making money.)

One boy who worked with Joseph in the first year remembered his accuracy and meticulous attention to detail, but even so the firm struggled throughout the 1870s and only just broke even. Progress was hampered by the lack of a van Houten press to make the good-quality cocoa that was being manufactured by Cadbury, and by Joseph's refusal to advertise.

What Joseph did do, however, was to try to poach workers and obtain manufacturing know-how from other chocolate factories. In 1872, he took out advertisements in London papers, some in the vicinity of Taylor's chocolate works. They asked for foremen and workmen who understood the manufacture of Rock and other cocoas and promised that applicants would be 'liberally dealt with'. Although this move has been labelled industrial espionage by some writers, Joseph perhaps saw it more as head-hunting. He had, after all, been saddled with an ailing business about which he knew very little, and by nature he was driven to acquire information and knowledge. Although the Rowntree name did not appear on the adverts (one told applicants to send a letter to 'G.F., 12 Bishopsgate St.'[8]), at least the advert was in the open, at a time when many chocolate manufacturers would plant moles to obtain their rivals' recipes and knowledge of their manufacturing processes.

As we saw in Chapter 2, the business finally turned around when Claude Gaget came on board in 1881 and was put in charge of the newly created French Confectionary Department, with the profits eventually enabling the purchase of a van Houten press and the launch of Elect Cocoa. As the workforce grew and production increased, it was increasingly apparent that Tanner's Moat was unsuitable. There were no lifts in the six-story building, so back injuries were common among the men who had to haul 10-stone sacks up flights of stairs. There were nowhere near enough cloakrooms and lavatories, and no way of providing hot food or even cups of tea. So in 1890, Joseph bought a site on Haxby Road just outside York. Like George Cadbury in 1878, he wanted a modern factory where workers could develop to their full potential. 'Healthful conditions of labour are not luxuries to be adopted or dispensed at will,' he insisted, 'They are conditions necessary for success.'[9]

Joseph also instigated various schemes for the benefit of his staff. Some reflected his concern with education. He established a library in about 1885 with £10 of his own money but deducted one penny a week from his employees for its upkeep. In 1891, he took the ground-breaking step of appointing a female overseer to take care of the girl staff's health and behaviour. Among other things, Miss Wood enforced a strict dress code of black dresses, after reprimanding one girl for wearing a blouse that exposed her throat. (This 'might easily draw a man's attention to you,' was her prim assessment.[10]) The first Rowntree doctor, who was Joseph's son-in-law, was appointed in 1904 (two years after the Cadburys had made a similar appointment), and on his advice a dentist followed. The firm also made pioneering advances in establishing a pension scheme. The aim was to provide a pension equal to at least half the wage a man was earning when he retired, which was ambitious given that such schemes were unchartered territory. To start things off, Joseph donated £10,000, which was supplemented by £9000 from the company and contributions from employees. Joseph also followed the Victorian tradition of organising an annual works outing. These were halted for some years, though, following a less than successful trip to Whitby: some employees elected to leave the train early and walk part of the way, and after being soaked in the rain they understandably headed to warm pubs to dry out. By the end of the day, they were so inebriated that they had to be escorted to the train by the police, which must have been mortifying for Joseph.

A further pioneering scheme was the *Cocoa Works Magazine* (*CWM*), launched in 1902. In the early days of Tanner's Moat, Henry and Joseph knew all the staff and were ready to step in if one of the workers was struggling with health or financial worries. The lines between work and personal life were occasionally blurred, as when, for example, Henry and Joseph provided cocoa and pork pies if overtime was required. Furthermore, the firm was small enough that employees knew how all the departments functioned and were invested in its success. As the firm grew, the 'family feel' was in danger of being lost. The *CWM* was an attempt to address this problem, and Joseph wrote in the first issue that 'if the business is to accomplish all that the Directors desire in combining social progress with commercial success, the entire body of workers must be animated by a common aim, and this will surely be furthered by a periodical devoted to matters of common interest'.[11] Along similar lines, an innovative 'suggestions scheme' was introduced for any suggestion, no matter how small, that might improve the manufacturing process, and the *CWM* regularly printed photos of winners receiving prizes.

After discussions with George Cadbury in 1900, Joseph bought 150 acres of land outside York and hired an architect to design a village on similar lines to Bournville. The ambition at New Earswick was to provide houses 'artistic in appearance, sanitary, well-built, and yet within the means of men earning about twenty-five shillings a week'.[12] Initially there were problems as the land was flat and uninteresting, there were no buses or streetlights, roads were rough, and families that moved there needed something of a pioneer spirit. In time, though, it included a Folk Hall, schools, playing fields, and parks. Although it proved impossible to provide houses for the lowest-income group, the village became a real community, partly because of the strength and vision of the Village Council.

Despite these developments and innovations, Joseph had not lost his passion for the statistical analysis of poverty. He was particularly troubled by the problems caused by alcohol. Quakers accepted all drink in moderation until 1835, at which point it was suggested that it might be desirable to abstain from distilled spirits. Wine and beer were considered innocuous if drunk with discretion, and until 1880 a few bottles of wine and beer appear in Joseph's annual domestic accounts. By 1897, however, he was advocating total abstinence and enlisted Arthur Sherwell to help him write a book, which was to be called *The Temperance Problem and Social Reform*. At first Joseph tried to write it in his summerhouse, which he referred to as his 'Temperance Den', but in an attempt to avoid distractions he later rented a house in Westow, a village 11 miles from York.

Investigators collected detailed figures, which were checked by experts on taxation and through government reports and conversations with bar-tenders. It was found that a large proportion of men on the edge of poverty spent about one-sixth of their income on beer and spirits. The book considered various solutions, analysing the pros and cons of 'dry states' in America and the 'company system' in operation in some towns in Sweden and Norway. In the latter, a company took over all bars in which spirits were sold, and managers received a fixed salary, thus removing the temptation to make profits by selling alcohol to customers who might be better off without it. Joseph favoured this sort of scheme, suggesting that the profits should be put into 'People's Palaces', a combination of art gallery, winter garden, concert hall, and temperance café, where people could socialise without drinking alcohol. Nothing came of his suggestion (even if the Government had been willing, the cost of buying the liquor trade would have been prohibitive), but, perhaps surprisingly, the nearly 700-page book, published in 1899, was a huge success—six editions were printed in the first eight months alone, and 90,000 copies sold in total. Joseph's son Seebohm, incidentally, used many of Joseph's statistics for a ground-breaking book in 1901 titled *Poverty: A Study of Town Life*, which played a part in the establishment of the welfare state.

Like George Cadbury, Joseph was troubled by excessive wealth and went some way to addressing his personal concerns by establishing three trusts in 1904. In relation to this, he wrote a private memorandum, 'The Opportunities and Dangers of Wealth', and sent copies to his children. He discussed how easy it was to acquire expensive habits step by step, which resulted in a barrier between the wealthy and their fellows, of how it was an act of great unkindness for parents to give their children everything they asked for, and of how considerable wealth often proved to be a curse rather than a blessing. 'In the remembrance of this,' he concluded, 'I have, with I believe the hearty assent of my children, given about one-half of my property to the establishment of three trusts.'[13] As mentioned above, the Village Trust was concerned with living conditions and houses at New Earswick. The Joseph Rowntree Charitable Trust was a social, charitable, and religious trust, with the purpose of financing social surveys, adult education, and activities of the Society of Friends. Finally, the Social Services Trust had similar aims to the charitable trust but did not have charitable status so had fewer legal restrictions on political work. Crucially, Joseph's aim with the latter two was to provide a means of investigating the *causes* rather than the *effects* of poverty. In a sentiment that is often quoted in philanthropic literature, he wrote, 'I feel that much of the current philanthropic effort is directed to remedying the more superficial manifestations of weakness or evil, while little thought or effort is directed to search out their underlying causes … Obvious distress or evil generally evokes so much feeling that the necessary agencies for alleviating it are pretty adequately supported … The Soup Kitchen in York never has difficulty in obtaining adequate financial aid, but an enquiry into the extent and causes of poverty would enlist little support.'[14] Tellingly, though, this seems to have been one area where Joseph did not follow his ideals—his personal accounts show that he regularly gave money to those who needed it, and that he was sensitive enough to be cryptic in recording the sums, for example, just writing 'Australian voyage of consumptive £10'.[15]

Joseph's main form of relaxation was walking. He spent many holidays in Mürren in the Swiss Alps, sometimes accompanied by one of his children and sometimes by a larger group. His weekly diversion was a Saturday walk in

Scarborough. He caught the 10 o'clock train from York, had a coffee at a café owned by a cousin, bought apples and ginger biscuits for lunch, walked, returned to the café at 4, and then went home. He stuffed a thin shabby mac in his pocket, and his only concession to luxury was two footwarmers prepared by a porter at the station. In the early years he went with his brother John, but later would ask a pupil from the Adult School or a factory worker. Some, understandably overawed, declined, but Joseph was good company. Sometimes he would probe factory workers about what they wanted from their job, and one young man remembered thinking that no one had ever taken so much trouble over him in his whole life before.

Joseph was also a bibliophile and built up a large library. As an apprentice he had made full use of his father's library, reading history, philosophy, Jane Austen, Charles Darwin, and John Stuart Mill. It was a habit that continued all his life, and once when asked about his prodigious memory for what he had read, he answered with disarming humility: 'I have made a practice of talking to the boys at meal times of the book I am reading. With such boys as I have, they cross-question me so much that I am forced to remember and to be ready for them at the next meal.'[16]

Indeed, although he could be strident and harsh in writing, especially over perceived injustices, Joseph was gentle in person, and it is said that he seldom gave a direct order: 'Should not this be...?' was a familiar beginning if he discovered something or someone in need of correction.[17] The Quaker and first Chief Medical Officer Sir George Newman attested that he was 'a patient listener, with a delightful sense of humour; he had the charm of humility and was both receptive and responsive.... [H]e mellowed like ripening fruit'.[18]

What about his faith? Joseph was a private man who seldom spoke of his own beliefs, and he is only known to have offered vocal ministry at Meeting once. That said, he undoubtedly lived a life that epitomized Quaker values. The Quaker testimonies of simplicity, peace, integrity, community, and equality were not set out as such until the 1940s, but Joseph avoided excessive luxury, valued integrity (as evidenced in his distaste for exaggerated advertising claims), campaigned for social justice for the wider community, and treated all people as equally valued.

Joseph was made an Honorary Freeman of the city of York in 1911, and he died on 24 February 1925. A measure of the esteem in which he was held can be gleaned from the coverage of his funeral in the northern edition of the *Daily Mirror*, which had a front-page spread of crowds of people walking past his grave, with the news that there had been an earthquake in New York relegated to a small box in the top corner.

George Cadbury and Joseph Rowntree clearly had much in common. Both had fathers with a passionate interest in social problems and lost their first wives. Both served as apprentices in the grocery trade at Pavement, went into the chocolate business with their brothers, taught at Adult Schools, built factories in the country with enlightened working conditions, provided leisure facilities for their employees, and established villages and trusts. George was first off the mark in business ventures, however. He seemed to thrive on struggle, whereas Joseph was more cautious and several times when he was older said it had never been his intention that the cocoa works should grow so large. Both arguably practised a benevolent paternalism, with neither permitting girls to work in the factory once they married, for example, George once explained that it would encourage their husbands to be lazy. Author Gillian Wagner says that a description of Joseph given by one of his workers might equally well have applied to George: ''E was very kind and very nice but ye couldn't get familiar with him. And if ye didn't give him a straight tale he made you feel like a little boy put under a table—but very nice and kind like.'[19] Both, though, undoubtedly left an inspiring and long-lasting legacy in terms of the chocolate works themselves, their wider impact on society, and the example they set their children. Next, we will see how this legacy was received by the next generation. First George's niece Beatrice, and then Joseph's son John Wilhelm.

Chapter 5

Beatrice Boeke: Anti-capitalist and pacifist

In August 1926, 42-year-old Beatrice, the daughter of Richard Cadbury, was entitled to an income of over £3000 a year from Cadbury share dividends, equivalent to about 20 times the average yearly wage. But rather than living the comfortable life of a wealthy heiress, Betty, as she was often known, was gaunt, white-haired, and homeless, camping in two borrowed ex-army tents in a wood near Bilthoven with her Dutch husband and six of her seven children. The story of how she ended up there is one of love, ideals, and a growing abhorrence of capitalism.

Richard's first wife, Elizabeth, had died in 1868, leaving him with four young children (Barrow, Jessie, William, and Richard Jr). A local widow, Mrs Emma Wilson, moved into the family home to help look after the children while also running, at Richard's behest, a creche for neglected children whose mothers were at work. Mrs Wilson's daughter Emma Jane was in Switzerland training to become a governess at the time, and when she was due to return home, it was agreed that she too would stay with the Cadburys until she found more permanent accommodation. She rang the doorbell as Richard happened to be passing through the hall, and when he opened it there was an instant mutual attraction. They were married less than a year later, in July 1871, and went on to have four girls (Edith, Helen, Daisy and Beatrice), with Beatrice inheriting her mother's cornflower blue eyes and English rose complexion. Barrow was 23 when Beatrice was born—they had a close bond and within the family were known as Big B and Little B.

Beatrice's early childhood was idyllic (with the possible exception of daily cold baths, which her mother insisted on for their health benefits). The family lived in Moseley Hall, a large and rambling mansion with vast grounds that included a garden teeming with rabbits and a bluebell wood. Richard would often send Beatrice and her nurse into town with armfuls of bluebells with instructions to give them away to children or anyone else who wanted them. Her fourth birthday present was a Shetland pony called Dolly. Weekdays began at 7.30 a.m. with a family breakfast, followed by a Bible reading and prayer, with the household being committed to God's care.

Home was undoubtedly a secure and happy place, but Beatrice was also exposed to the effects of poverty. Richard organized day trips to Moseley Hall for the children of the Birmingham slums, and when they arrived, ragged, often shoeless, and with unwashed matted hair, he would oversee the preparation of milky hot chocolate and buns while instructing his children to raid their cupboards for toys. In 1891, however, Richard and Emma Jane decided to hand over their home to be converted into a convalescent centre for children, and the family moved into a nearby house that Richard had designed named Uffculme. It had a very different feel from Moseley Hall, with stuffed birds along the walls of the vast hall and Richard's souvenirs from his travels in every available space, and Beatrice hated it.

For her early education, Beatrice attended a kindergarten run according to the German Froebel method. Unusually for Victorian England, it was child-centred and experiential. At 11, she started at Edgbaston High School, where she loved playing hockey and was described in reports as diligent and intelligent. Outside the classroom, her education continued through Richard's love of travel, with trips to France, Switzerland and Italy introducing her to fine art, history, and different cultures. One particularly memorable holiday was a tour of Egypt and Palestine in 1897, when Beatrice crawled through narrow, dusty passages in the Great Pyramid, swam in the Dead Sea, camped (in luxury) under stunning desert stars, and visited the biblical sites of Bethel and Damascus.

In 1899 the Nile trip was repeated, but this time Beatrice, Helen and Richard contracted what the locals called Nile throat. They were held up for a week in Cairo until declared well enough to travel and then set off for Jerusalem. But by the time they arrived, Richard had relapsed and his throat was agony. In the early hours of the morning the girls were woken by their mother and summoned to his bedside, where they found their father unconscious. He had suffered a heart attack and never recovered: Nile throat turned out to be diphtheria.

Amidst the outpouring of grief from the press and Bournville workers, the business repercussions of Richard's death were made slightly smoother because shortly before the trip a succession plan had been put into place. It had been decided that should one of the brothers die, the partnership would be turned into a limited company. George and his sons Edward and George Jr, and Richard's sons Barrow and William formed the new team of directors, and ordinary and preference shares were issued. Preference shares gave a fixed dividend every year but carried no voting power, and ordinary shares came with voting power but could not be transferred to anyone outside the Cadbury family. Beatrice was almost 16 at the time, and her shares were put in trust until she was 21.

In 1901, Beatrice started to board at the Quaker Mount School in York. The school had links with the Quaker Bootham school for boys and was again a trailblazer in education. Beatrice joined the Natural History Society, the Debating Society, the Poetry Learning Association and the Astronomical Society, and excelled at the violin. She was clearly very sociable — she enjoyed partying, sending home for her 'white silk skirts', and in her report, her head of bedroom remarked 'Has tried hard, yet bedroom sometimes noisy and untidy'.[1] Letters to her mother reveal an affectionate nature: 'I do love thee so, and I think of thee and dearest daddy all the time.'[2] Academically, it seems there were too many distractions for Beatrice to reach her true potential, but she managed to gain entry to the women-only Westfield College, which was affiliated with the University of London. The partying and requests for clothes continued, but Beatrice was beginning to take an interest in social issues, attending a lecture on poverty by C. F. G. Masterman, who had written a book in 1901 on the problems of modern city life. She was also inspired by the ground-breaking women around her. When one of her tutors became only the second woman to be awarded a D. Litt, a delighted Beatrice wrote home that 'we chaired her round the dining hall to "Hail the conquering hero comes"'.[3]

After finishing at Westfield, Beatrice returned to Uffculme to keep her mother company, and in 1906 the two of them planned a round-the-world trip to see Beatrice's sisters. Helen had married a well-known Tennessee singer and evangelist called Charles Alexander, and the couple travelled widely. (She had met him while helping her mother serve refreshments when he was preaching in Birmingham.) Daisy had married a doctor, Neville Bradley, who was running a leper colony in southern China under the auspices of the Friends Foreign Mission Association (FFMA). Appropriately for a Quaker missionary who would have been familiar with the idea of the inward light of God, Neville was referred to as 'I shang', or 'Healing light'. The party all met up at Daisy and Neville's, and Beatrice was deeply impressed by her tour of the colony, which was clean and provided opportunities for the patients to buy medicine by making and selling goods.

Emma Jane and Beatrice continued from China to Japan and then boarded the SS Oceania for Vancouver. During the crossing there was a violent storm, and Emma Jane tumbled down a flight of stairs, hitting her head. She drifted in and out of consciousness during the night, but the injury proved fatal. Beatrice's shock and grief for the rest of the voyage were compounded by a fever suspected to be pneumonia. In Canada, she stayed with Helen and Charles, who were on tour in Winnipeg, while arranging to transport the body home, an ordeal that surely must have brought back memories of her father's death abroad. The sisters then returned to Birmingham to sort out their mother's affairs. Charles and Helen had built a house called Tennessee in the grounds of Uffculme a few years earlier, and it was decided that Beatrice would move in with them.

So at 23, Beatrice found herself wealthy and in possession of a good education, but single, parentless, and without a clear direction in life. She picked up some of Emma Jane's charitable work in Birmingham, and then at Charles and Helen's invitation joined them on a round-the-world preaching tour, where she witnessed the 'transformational' effect of mission work. The intrepid Beatrice travelled home on her own, a journey that included two weeks on the Trans-Siberian railway, and decided that mission work was her destiny. Back in Birmingham, she accepted an invitation to serve on the FFMA Candidates Committee, responsible for appointing missionaries.

In 1910, the Committee was tasked with finding a head teacher for the Boy's High School in Brummana in Syria (later Lebanon). One of the applicants was a tall, blue-eyed, engineering doctoral student from Alkmaar in Holland. Cornelis Boeke went by the nickname of Kees (pronounced 'Case'). He was from a Mennonite family but was drawn to the Society of Friends and mission work, especially in education. His sincerity impressed Beatrice and he was offered the job, which involved spending a year training at Woodbrooke. In early 1911, Beatrice formed a study circle to which Kees was invited, and a brief but intense courtship followed, fuelled by ardent letters ('Friendship comes unasked and cannot be rejected,' wrote Kees, 'no forces can possibly keep it out, when once its tyrant-will has decided to get in!'[4]). Kees proposed in early July, and an initially hesitant Beatrice accepted a fortnight later, realizing that they had common beliefs and ideals. Beatrice was planning a holiday in Cornwall with Helen and Charles, and Kees invited himself and a friend along (staying, of course, in separate accommodation). He was an accomplished violinist and had promised to practise so he could play Bach to Beatrice, especially the tremendous *Ciaccona*, which he pronounced the finest piece ever written for solo violin. Beatrice bought Kees a violin costing £100 (£10,000 in 2023) as an engagement present.

Kees went out to Syria in September, returning to marry on 19 December, and the couple then travelled back in a leisurely manner, via Alkmaar to visit Kees' mother, then Paris, Marseille, Cairo, Beirut, and finally to Brummana. They took bulky luggage, including a dining-room suite and piano that were transported by camel. ('There can hardly have been more upsetting episodes in the life either of the piano, or of the camel!' remarked one of their friends.[5]) Their living conditions were simple though—one large room with a curtain to divide off the sleeping area, with most meals taken with the boys at long tables.

Beatrice gave birth to her first child, Helen, on 11 November 1912, but a few days later she was desperately ill with a fever and delirium: she was diagnosed as having typhoid, which had probably been lying dormant for months. Barrow sent over a nurse, and Daisy's doctor husband came over with another nurse, but it was three months before Beatrice was well enough to see Helen, a meeting at which they both cried. By 1914, however, Beatrice was pregnant again, so in view of that and the outbreak of war the couple decided to heed advice and travel back to England, enduring a dangerous sea voyage undertaken at night in blackout conditions.

Figure 5: Beatrice, Kees and baby Helen in 1913 (public domain)

Once home, the family moved into Helen and Charles' Tennessee home, and Emma was born on 21 November. Beatrice settled into the lifestyle of many other women of her background—breakfast in bed, shopping at Liberty for clothes for the baby, and entertaining afternoon visitors. The war, however, was forcing many Quakers to think through their attitude towards the peace testimony. While some Quakers maintained a pacifist stance and refused to be involved in any way, others joined relief efforts, and still others concluded that fighting for the greater good of humankind or to defend their country was permissible. Egbert (Bertie) Cadbury (George's youngest son), for example, enlisted in the navy and later joined the Royal Air Force, once piloting a plane that made a daring night-time sortie to shoot down Zeppelins approaching Great Yarmouth. His brother Laurence, by contrast, undertook relief work with the Friends' Ambulance Service. Kees and Beatrice, for their part, became involved with the Fellowship of Reconciliation (FOR), which boasted members from various denominations. Kees was made secretary of the Birmingham branch, and, as he was a Dutch national and Holland was neutral, he was asked to travel to Germany to contact German anti-war campaigners. Although he had Beatrice's enthusiastic support, the rest of the family advised caution. The trip was a success, however. Kees was abroad from July to September and met many prominent pacifists.

By 1915, Kees was teaching at The Woodruffs, a private school, and Beatrice gave birth to a third girl, Paula, in January 1916. By now, aware of the suffering being faced in some places in Europe and that some of their Syrian friends were literally starving, she was beginning to question her lavish lifestyle. And both she and Kees were becoming increasingly involved in pacifist activities. Kees was forced to resign after he told his pupils that Jesus had commanded us to love our enemies and that the Germans were our brothers; however, he continued to proclaim from street corners that man was not made to kill man. Beatrice assisted him even though she was once more pregnant: Julia was born in June 1917. In January 1918, the family moved to Wales so that Kees could mobilise the growing anti-war feeling. While there, he received a summons to appear in Birmingham Law Courts on 17 February 1918 in relation to previous street preaching, his message being deemed likely to interfere with the success of His Majesty's forces. Kees argued that much of what he said was in line with the teaching of Jesus, but he was found guilty, imprisoned, and, much to the family's surprise and dismay, deported on 8 April. Beatrice and the children were finally granted permission to join him in July. The journey started stressfully, as the hard-won travel permit fluttered from Beatrice's fingers in a gust of wind the evening before the ship was due to sail, but to her relief a policeman arrived a few hours later with a replacement. The crossing itself was miserable. Beatrice clutched the baby while keeping the three older children together with a long set of reins, and Emma, Paula and Julia were dreadfully seasick.

Once in Holland, the couple bought a house called *Het Boschhuis* (the house in the woods) in Bilthoven, near Utrecht, with funds from Beatrice's inheritance. It had three large rooms and a kitchen on the ground floor, six bedrooms, two attic rooms and a covered porch, and was surrounded by pine trees. In line with their growing awareness of wealth inequality, however, the furnishings were only the simplest and most necessary. Beatrice learned Dutch and her warm-hearted manner meant that she made friends easily. Shortly after the war ended, the couple helped to found an organization translated as the Brotherhood of Christ with the aim of uniting pacifist groups all over Holland. They also organized an international conference for pacifists at *Het Boschhuis*: the outcome was the formation of the International Fellowship of Reconciliation (IFOR), with Kees appointed as joint secretary.

Kees continued to preach his message in the public squares of Utrecht, despite having had his application to do so rejected. Beatrice, now expecting her fifth child, gave out pamphlets and took her turn at speaking. When she was eight months pregnant, however, they were both arrested and sent to prison—Beatrice for two weeks and Kees for three. Suffering from claustrophobia in her cell, Beatrice tried to keep her spirits up by singing hymns, hoping that Kees would hear, but was soon told to stop.

Against the backdrop of these events, Beatrice was questioning her right to the dividends from her Cadbury's shares. (As we saw, they were £3000 a year after tax, at a time when a skilled factory operator at Bournville earned less than £150 per year.) In August 1920, she and Kees travelled to Switzerland, having arranged to meet the Christian socialist Professor Leonhard Ragaz to discuss the matter. It appears to have been at this meeting that she came to the decision to relinquish her shares in Cadbury and give them to the workers at Bournville so that they could use the dividends to promote causes of peace and internationalism.

It was a gift that was to prove extremely difficult to give. Beatrice initially wrote to Barrow to inform him of her decision and was immediately summoned to Birmingham. Of course, she was aware that her uncle, brothers and cousins were in many ways exemplary employers, but fired by her investigations into Marxism and socialism, she maintained that capitalism was at the root of war: capitalist leaders let their riches pile up and enjoyed lives of privilege, which fuelled the strife between the 'haves' and 'have-nots' and ultimately ended in conflicts such as the Great War. She put her case to Barrow and three other directors, all dressed soberly in black suits, in the wood-panelled boardroom, and they pointed out a number of obstacles: ordinary shares could not be legally passed to anyone outside the family because they carried voting power; the legacy was not just for Beatrice but also for her children;

and the Cadburys could hardly be accused of neglecting their civic duty.

Beatrice stayed in Birmingham after the meeting, as Helen's husband had recently died from a stroke, and two weeks later she received a letter from Tom Hackett, the Bournville Works' foreman. Educated and articulate, Tom agreed that the competitive system of industry was wrong, but he felt that change should come about slowly, through education. Beatrice's gesture, he argued, would not change the relationship between capital and labour. Furthermore, less than 10 per cent of the workforce would be in sympathy with her ideals, and handing over the use of so much money to a group of people regardless of their outlook in life would not achieve the end she had in mind.

The wrangling continued as Beatrice returned to Bilthoven. At this point, the couple were considering the radical step of withdrawing from the Dutch state, which they claimed was an 'institution of violence'. They set up the Bilthoven Community Council to tackle local issues such as the lack of social housing, and Beatrice, in a bold move, wrote to the workers at Birmingham saying that if they did not want the money, she would give it to the new Bilthoven Council. The letter focused minds, and Tom Hackett and Kathleen Cox (from the Women's Works' Council) visited Bilthoven and concluded that Beatrice's money would be better off in Bournville than with those 'Dutch visionaries'. The pair noted, however, that the Boekes were putting themselves in a position in which the family would have to exist on the money earned by Kees, 'probably as a carpenter'. (Kees did indeed subsequently spend some time learning the trade and building staircases in Utrecht.) The legal complexities were solved when Beatrice was advised to transfer her shares to a trust so that the income could be donated to various causes by Cadbury employees during her lifetime, but her children would receive the capital on her death. The Boeke Trust was duly set up. To be consistent, Beatrice handed over the ownership of *Het Boschhuis* to the Quaker Meeting in Bilthoven, although the family continued to live there, growing vegetables and keeping hens for eggs. Beatrice had her sixth child, her only son, named Daniel, in November 1921.

Kees and Beatrice were also aware of tax resistance as a form of political activism, and now Kees wrote to Queen Wilhelmina to say that they would pay tax but withhold the amount used for military purposes (thought to be 42 per cent). When the Queen failed to reply, they stopped paying taxes altogether, and soon the tax bill plus interest and fines came to £400. The authorities therefore ordered a forced sale of their assets, set for 25 March 1922. Many household items were sold, along with Kees' piano and the valuable violin. Seemingly undaunted, Kees and Beatrice attended a public meeting in Utrecht that evening, and when they returned found that some friends had made makeshift furniture from packing boxes and hung blankets over the windows. Word reached Birmingham, however, and a few days later Barrow and his wife, Geraldine, arrived and insisted on replacing some essential items.

Barely two months later though, Kees wrote a pamphlet titled 'Break with the State'. From now on, they would pay no tax, make no pension contributions, surrender their passports (because they viewed national boundaries as inherently divisive), and make no use of the railways or postal service, which were both state-owned institutions. They also renounced any claim for help from the police. Furthermore, since they no longer believed in owning property, they instigated an 'open door' policy at *Het Boschhuis*. The door-locks were removed, and anyone was free to stay or take what they needed.

Kees and Beatrice's extreme actions inevitably sent ripples through their community. Their relationship with the Fellowship of Reconciliation cooled, partly because the organization was disappointed that some of the share money had not been allocated for their work. Moreover, wanting to be aligned with those who believed in humanitarianism first and foremost, the couple drifted away from the Brotherhood of Christ and, in a move that shocked Birmingham relatives, resigned their membership from the Society of Friends.

Meanwhile, back in Birmingham there was inevitably concern about how the Boekes were living, from both family and the trustees of the Boeke Trust. Beatrice refused to accept any help from the Trust, but the trustees were not above subterfuge, and in fact Kathleen and Tom had taken the precaution of persuading some of the Boeke's Dutch friends to accept money from the trust to provide essentials surreptitiously. Beatrice believed that the occasional gifts of food left on the doorstep came from the unprompted generosity of friends.

Beatrice had her seventh child, Theodora, on 27 March 1923. Photos show her as desperately thin, with her white hair swept up in a bun. The couple's political activism continued unabated, however. Kees, who was now giving English and violin lessons, decided to stop using money, and Beatrice, after an initial period during which she collected fees, followed suit a year later. By this time, they had many detractors and were often dismissed as cranks.

The Boeke children, meanwhile, were attending the Montessori school in Bilthoven. It was fee-paying, but the head was sympathetic to the Boekes and waived the fees. In 1925 though, a new law was passed stating that all fees had to be paid through the local authority rather than directly to the school. The Boekes' 'Break with the State' stance left them with no option other than to remove the children from the school. Kees, ever resourceful, decided to set up his own school for his children in a friend's spare room. His aim was to become a catalyst for learning rather than to impose his will.

The situation at *Het Boschhuis* continued to be precarious: people were continuously coming and going, the walls were grimy, basic kitchen utensils were missing, and the once fine library was ruined (several valuable first editions had turned up in bookshops in Utrecht). In August 1926, an already difficult living situation became untenable when some vagrants moved in and took over the ground floor. The Boekes couldn't ask the police for help because they had broken with the state. They couldn't go to Birmingham because they had renounced their passports. And they couldn't write to the Cadburys, even if they had wanted to, because they were not using the postal service. Forced to leave their home, they accepted the offer of the loan of two tents from a friend and camped at Den Dolder, an area dotted with pine trees and sandy hillocks. The first two months were fun, something of an adventure, but October was unusually wet, the tents leaked, and one child was sleeping under an umbrella. Word again reached Birmingham, and once more Barrow and Geraldine came over. They found the children dirty and forlorn, three-year-old Theodora shoeless, and Candia probably anaemic. (Did Beatrice ever think back to the children of the Birmingham slums she had encountered at Moseley Hall?) Sensitive to the Boekes' idealism and eminently diplomatic, Barrow and Geraldine found a small cottage for them to rent in the working-class quarter of Bilthoven and helped them retrieve their few remaining possessions from *Het Boschhuis*.

The next decade was calmer, with the Boekes' former extremism tempered by experience, perhaps. It was not without further health issues though. Beatrice, aged 43, was pregnant again, and following the birth was seriously ill for weeks with inflammation of the kidneys. Kees, however, building on his teaching and home-schooling experience, had found his vocation. Both he and Beatrice had become convinced that change to society had to start with the education of children, who should learn about love, fellowship, and respect for others. With the help of a donation from the Boeke Trust, a new school was built, and Kees named it *De Werkplaats Kindergemeenschap* (the Children's Community Workshop). There were no grades so as to eliminate competition, the children undertook cleaning duties, and play and outdoor activity were nurtured. Beatrice taught English and acted as a warm mother figure to the children. By 1936 the school had 100 pupils and 9 full-time and 18 part-time teachers. A decade later, Princess Juliana, the Queen's daughter, would return from her war-time exile in Canada and send the young princesses Beatrix, Irene and Margriet to the school. (They too had to clean but were driven to school in a Cadillac sedan with their bodyguards.)

It was during the war that Kees and Beatrice had a rare difference in opinion. In 1942, all schools in Holland were ordered to give the names of non-Aryan children to the occupiers. While Kees and others felt that compliance was necessary to keep the school open and that the children were in no danger, Beatrice saw it as a betrayal of community. She argued that closing the school first would show solidarity with the Jewish children and avoid reprisals. Failing to convince others, she withdrew cooperation from the school and taught some of the Jewish children at home and at a friend's house. The Boekes also offered sanctuary to two Jewish children, Norman (9) and Anita (6) Magnus, who changed their names to Jan and Liesje Wachness. The names of Beatrice and Kees are now inscribed on the wall of honour at the Yad Vashem Museum in Jerusalem as being among the 'Righteous Among the Nations'.

Once 'retired', the Boekes spent eight months in Lebanon trying to raise money for a community for refugee children, but they were unsuccessful, and both suffered from ill health. Returning home, they settled in Abcoude, just outside Amsterdam. Having earlier renounced membership of the Society of Friends, Beatrice became a much-valued member of the Amsterdam meeting. Kees died in 1966, and Beatrice on 13 February 1976 at age 91. Her obituary paid tribute to a loving woman who saw the best in everyone.

Chapter 6

John Wilhelm Rowntree: Quaker reformer

Once, when John was asked 'Which Rowntree are *you*?', he quipped 'Oh, the brother of Poverty and the son of Drink'.[1] He was of course referring to the books written by his relatives, but John was widely admired in his own right, especially for his gentle courage in the face of chronic illness and for his vision of a liberal Quakerism that embraced modern thought and emphasized an inner experience of Christ. As a boy, however, there was little evidence of the man he would become.

As we saw in Chapter 4, Joseph Rowntree's first wife, Julia, died in 1863, four months after the birth of Lilley, and in 1867 he married Julia's cousin Antoinette, known as Tonie. From a distance of more than a century and only patchy accounts, it seems an unlikely match. Joseph was thoroughly invested in English Quakerism, measured, studious, and serious. Tonie was from a German family and not a Quaker, and although she later became a member of the Society, she never took an active part in its life. Furthermore, she enjoyed painting and playing the piano, activities that had traditionally been viewed with suspicion among Quakers and that were only just becoming acceptable. Tonie had a strained relationship with the Rowntrees at times, and many people were reportedly afraid of her, including the servants as she was an exacting mistress. She was, apparently, a woman whose reactions were generally unpredictable. John Wilhelm was the first child of this second marriage, born in 1868. He had a German nurse and spoke German before he spoke English.

John inherited his mother's aptitude for art, especially in pen and ink work, although he made little use of this gift outside illustrations for his Adult School lessons. He also, perhaps, inherited something of her temperament. He was 'very passionate and easily aroused,' his sister Agnes recalled, 'I think Seebohm and I rather feared his outbursts at one time—they were so violent. On one occasion (I think he was about twelve years old and at Bootham School) he bit a lady who was living with us at the time, so badly in the arm, that she bore the mark for years!'[2] Reports from school do not paint a much brighter picture. In what sounds like a diplomatic understatement, one schoolmaster recounted that he 'was undoubtedly a boy of good natural ability but being far from robust had never learned to use it effectively. He was not of a happy, contented disposition'.[3] Alongside any possibly inherited character traits, part of John's problem was undoubtedly that, in addition to not being 'robust', he was already going deaf and by nine was having to use an ear trumpet, which must have been frustrating: another schoolmaster recalled that John would always sit by him in order to be able to hear, and follow him to the blackboard.

John left school in 1886 and joined the family business at the ramshackle Tanner's Moat factory. He started at the bottom, doing manual work in each department. He was often irritable if over-tired, but even so reportedly won the friendship and esteem of the employees. He became a partner at 21 and was heavily involved in the plans to move to Haxby Road. In 1892 he married Constance Naish, a capable woman who initially turned down his proposal because she was considering studying maths or music at college. It was by all accounts a happy and close marriage, and the couple would go on to have four daughters and one son.

Despite this seemingly successful life, however, John was undergoing a spiritual crisis. In this he was not alone. The end of the nineteenth century was a tumultuous period for many Christians, especially young, educated ones. Darwin's theories had not been integrated into Christianity (*On the Origin of Species* was published in 1859), and the advent of 'higher criticism' was casting doubt on the historical reliability of the Bible. John might have failed to distinguish himself academically at school, but he had a restless, inquisitive mind and was challenged by new discoveries. The crisis started, he recalled, with the realization that he doubted that Jesus raised Lazarus from the dead. 'I think I woke up simply to find that I had never really believed anything,' he wrote in a letter in 1893. 'I gave up one thing after another gradually, without any heart-rending or regret.'[4] A period of agnosticism followed, and he admitted that if he had not been so 'favourably circumstanced' he would have left the Friends.

Spiritual help came through Dr Richard H. Thomas from Baltimore, who made a religious visit to England in 1889/90. In later years, Richard would write a book of religious poetry, *Echoes and Pictures*, and a charming novel called *Penelve: Among the Quakers* about a progressive Quaker community in Pennsylvania. His views exemplified the American strand of Quakerism that embraced modern thought, as against the evangelical strand that strove to maintain more traditional formulations of faith. From Richard, John discovered that there was nothing to fear from the progress of knowledge. This was partly because new knowledge would shed light on faith, stripping away false beliefs. It was also because Christ became a life-giving spirit for him, an ever-present guiding inward spirit of life rather than merely a historical figure in the Bible. A flavour of Richard's message can be gleaned from an address he gave in 1895: 'We are to live in the power of God, as in the atmosphere around us. We are to feed on God, and to know His power, not only as outside, but as within us. The iron is in the fire; but leave it there long enough, and the fire is the iron. That is what we want, to so yield ourselves up to the Lord Jesus that He may be in us, and we in Him.'[5] After Richard's death, John wrote a heartfelt letter to his widow, Anna, confiding that 'He was to me a dear and intimate friend, and one who at a critical time in my own religious experience gave me, more than any one person I know, the help which I needed'.[6] John's faith had moved from being a series of intellectual doubts to a deeply personal experience coupled with the confidence that science and biblical studies would strip away erroneous beliefs but leave the truth.

By 1893, at age 24, John was eager to share his revitalized faith with the Society at large, and especially with younger Quakers. He spoke at Yearly Meeting in London, pleading for understanding from older Quakers for the difficulties faced by younger ones who could not accept older expressions of faith. He wanted all to be assured that those things that were of God would stand and those that were not would fall away. He came away stimulated and wrote to a friend, 'I see more what is wanted, and feel more determined than ever to devote my life to making the Society of Friends, as far as my little power and little scope allow, a real and living force in the world.'[7] About a month later, he wrote a pamphlet titled 'A few thoughts upon the position of young Friends in relation to the Society', which expanded on his talk and generated a vast amount of correspondence. John's uncle, John Stevenson, was initially perturbed, but once it became clear that his nephew would not merely be critical but powerfully and vitally reconstructive, he gave him his unreserved support.

Also in 1893, John, who had been teaching at the Adult School in York with his father since he left school, struck out with his friend Edward Worsdell to establish a new school in the nearby village of Acomb. The students included many railway employees, and the sessions would begin with a hymn, followed by a pause for silent prayer, and then a portion of the Bible read round by the men. Next, John would unfold some aspect of the natural world and apply it to the passage. For example, his notebooks give details of a talk on geology, leading to a spiritual conclusion: 'Geological examination of ourselves will reveal that our character is a stratified rock, each day laying a layer.... Life is made up of hundreds of little microscopic decisions between right and wrong.'[8]

As this sense of mission was opening though, John's health took a turn for the worse. Progressive blindness had been predicted in 1891, and in 1894 he went to London to consult specialists. There he was given the devastating news that before he reached middle age, he would be totally blind and deaf. There was no cure, and the disease was life-threatening. Some accounts of his life mention a rare kidney disease that would also rob him of his memory, but it is not clear what he knew when. (He was certainly diagnosed with retinitis pigmentosa by the specialists, which can be associated with kidney disease and loss of hearing in some syndromes, although these had not been identified at the time.) Rufus Jones, who would become a close friend and reforming partner a few years later, wrote of what John told him of that life-changing news in London: 'Dazed and overwhelmed by the diagnosis he staggered from the doctor's office to the street and stood there holding on to a post on the curb. Suddenly he felt the love of God flow around him and through him as though a visible presence with everlasting arms enfolded him, and immediately a joy filled him, such as he had never known before.'[9] After his English doctors told him they could not help, John found a doctor in Chicago who was trying an experimental treatment for his eye disease, and over the coming years visited him regularly. The treatment involved having strychnine injected into his veins, which made his arms jump and twitch for hours afterwards.

The following year, keen to see as much as possible before his sight failed completely, John and some friends travelled to Egypt and Palestine. He had the ability to bring a scene to life in just a few words, and in his journal wrote of evening camp life, when the heat of the day was forgotten and the glaring hills had softened to a mysterious violet. Then, he recorded, with self-deprecating humour, 'We accept our dragoman's invitation, and squatting down Arab fashion among our cooks and muleteers, drink the coffee of friendship with them. Then come the jokes at our remissness in rising, how often we had to be called, and the time we take to dress, and the things we leave in the tent.'[10]

Back in Britain, the changes that had been set in motion in 1893 reached something of a tipping point at the Manchester Conference of 1895. It was an event attended by over a thousand Quakers (out of a membership of about 16,500) and is generally accepted as putting British Quakerism on a path that would embrace 'modern thought', a liberal theology, and social engagement. The opening speech, prepared by Matilda Sturge but read in her absence by her niece Helen Sturge, stated the challenges clearly: 'We live in an age of science, and its discoveries have brought new difficulties for those who have trusted in the verbal and literal inspiration of the Bible; we live in an age of criticism, and criticism has dared to examine the Bible.'[11] Papers presented over the next four days covered subjects such as the relationship of Quakerism to science and social issues, the presentation of spiritual truth, and the message of Quakerism for the world.

John's address was one of four papers delivered on 12 November on the subject 'Has Quakerism a message for the world today?'[12] He did not hide his despair over the current state of Quakerism, dramatically declaring that 'the empty benches and deserted galleries of our meeting-houses are signs of a high-water mark from which the tide has ebbed away'. He identified three problems and their solution. The first was the indifference to the 'higher life' occasioned by the attraction of public-houses and music-halls and the quest for money. The solution here was spiritual: 'O Christ, convince us by Thy Spirit ... lay on us the burden of the world's suffering.' The second was the change in religious thought, as the truth about humans and their affinities with all other forms of life was being made known. Here John was confident that there would 'spring out of this present seeming chaos, a renewed and more powerful faith, deeper in its basis, clearer in its vision, broader in its charity, than ever was the old; *and as warm in its love'*. The third was the changes in society wrought by the Industrial Revolution and the growing challenge to the traditional view that inequalities of wealth were the ordering of Divine providence. Here John saw a two-fold solution: Quakers should continue their established work in the slums and Adult Schools, but also consider, in dependence on God, how they could reach the lawyers and journalists of Fleet Street and the baronets and dukes of Piccadilly.

The challenges of modern thought were being felt across the Atlantic too. Here, the leading voice for theological modernization was that of Rufus Jones, a charismatic lecturer at Haverford College in Philadelphia, who was five years older than John. He had a deep personal and academic interest in mysticism, which he defined as an everyday, usually undramatic experience of God—something that chimed with John's emphasis on the experience of Christ within. In the next decade, Rufus would go on to argue that this experience was consistent with the new science of psychology being advanced by William James and with the latest developments in philosophy. In 1895, however, he was just starting his career as a lecturer and editor of the Quaker journal *The American Friend*. He had not attended the Manchester Conference but was informed of it in a letter from Henry Stanley Newman, editor of the British Quaker journal *The Friend*. Henry wrote that it was the first attempt of the Society to come to terms with modern thought and a vital effort to retain highly educated and intelligent young men and women belonging to the best old Quaker families.

These two young visionary leaders met for the first time two years later, in 1897, in the Swiss Alps. John had holidayed in Mürren with Joseph when he was 15, and this year father and son were there as part of a group of about a dozen. Rufus had been in England, where he had attended Yearly Meeting, visited English Quakers, and enjoyed a tour of the Cadbury chocolate factory. To finish off his trip, he and Rendel Harris, a respected biblical scholar, planned a walking holiday to coincide with the Rowntrees in Mürren. The rain had been relentless, the bed bugs had been vicious, and Rufus' mood was low. But everything was about to change. The day after they arrived was a Sunday, so one of the rooms was requisitioned for a Meeting for Worship, which Rufus described as 'heavenly'. In the afternoon, as the rain continued to batter against the windows, Rufus and John realized not only that they shared a vision for the future of Quakerism but that they were kindred spirits. They discussed John's plans for summer schools, a permanent Quaker settlement for education, an ambitious multi-volume history of Quakerism, and a thoughtful, fearless magazine for the modern Quaker point of view.

The weather cleared overnight, and the next morning they rose at 2 a.m. to join a guided hike to see dawn from the summit of the 10,000-ft Schilthorn. Walking arm in arm because of John's failing sight they continued to plan, before enjoying breakfast at the top and an exhilarating sledge down the mountain on burlap sacks. 'We both knew before the day was over,' wrote Rufus, 'that we were to be comrades for the rest of life.'[13]

Over the next few years, John began to put the ideas he had discussed with Rufus into action. The plans for summer schools were already underway. The first took place in August 1897 and was attended by 400 women and 259 men. Topics were wide-ranging, including social problems, the New Testament, early Hebrew poetry, and the difference between the Socratic and the Christian standpoints. The schools would continue for a couple of decades. Then, in 1898 he launched *Present Day Papers*. The thrust of the journal was that yesterday's truth was ineffective unless it was reborn in the heart of the new generation. Each year's issues were attractively bound with an apt line from the

Quaker poet John Greenleaf Whittier on the title page: 'And all the windows of my heart I open to the day.' Leading Friends contributed, but also non-Quakers, such as W. R. Inge, the Dean of St Paul's and a scholar of mysticism.

Also in 1898, John wrote an article in *The Friend* arguing that the absence of ministers meant that all Quakers shared the burden of teaching, so education was key. The following year, his article in *Present Day Papers* outlined a vision for a Quaker settlement. It would be a place that would be a centre for the diffusion of religious knowledge where ordinary people could learn from university teachers, a training ground for social service, and a source of spiritual fellowship. As we saw in Chapter 3, George Cadbury had been convinced while out riding that he should offer Woodbrooke as the home for this venture. Meanwhile, across the Atlantic, Rufus' first wife, Sallie, had died of tuberculosis and he had married Elizabeth Cadbury (from the American side of the Cadbury family). Both George and John were keen for Rufus to take up the post of principal at Woodbrooke, but after much thought and discussion he wrote to decline the offer, believing he could do more good in America. 'It is idle to pretend that your letter is anything other than a severe blow!' replied a disappointed John.[14] The post was subsequently taken up by Rendel Harris.

By 1899, John's deteriorating health meant he was advised to retire from the cocoa works and move to the country. The family settled in Scalby, near Scarborough, and John took up gardening (aiming to 'intensify cabbages', as he put it). He remained on the board though, and occasionally travelled abroad on business. The first volume of the *Cocoa Works Magazine* detailed one memorable trip made in 1901, when he and Constance were aboard the steamer *Para*, which was bringing back cocoa from Trinidad and Granada. Some bananas were also being transported, using an experimental method that attempted to avoid deterioration by extracting oxygen from the storage containers. It was not a success: in John's words, 'There was an appalling roar, a momentary flash followed by blinding darkness. Mrs R and myself found ourselves hurled into the air ... ship's officers and crew behaved as Englishmen should ... the captain, while in the air, shouted for the Fire Brigade.'[15]

In preparation for his grand project of writing the history of Quakerism, John had collected over 2000 books and pamphlets. He had mapped the series out and anticipated that it would take 10 years to write. But this was one vision he would not see through. On 13 February 1905, Joan Fry wrote a letter to Rufus: 'We have just had a delightful visit of one night from J.W.R. He most kindly came to lecture in our tiny Meeting House... & we are all feeling refreshed & uplifted by his presence & his words. It is sad for us that he has to go off to America just now, but you may benefit somewhat by our loss.'[16] John was coming to see his Chicago eye doctor, and Rufus had written to invite him to stay: 'We are still hoping that the next letter will tell us to "cool off" one of our rooms for an English visitor from the Yorkshire moors! We will have water in the pitcher duly frozen and the wind shall blow across the bed all night!' he teased.[17] John and Constance set sail aboard the *Caronia*, but by the time the ship docked in New York, John was desperately ill with pneumonia. Fortunately, Rufus had arranged to meet them so was able to help with getting him to hospital. John's kidneys had failed and he was delirious, refusing to believe that Rufus was the 'real Rufus'. He died on 9 March and was buried at Haverford eight days later. The only comfort his friends could take from the tragedy was that the Chicago doctor came to the funeral and told them that the treatment was ineffective, so John had been spared the slow but irresistible weakening of his sight and intellectual powers. As regards the history project, the seven-volume series was written mainly by Rufus and William Charles Braithwaite.

Following his death, many tributes were paid to John, sometimes in extravagant language, and his memory came to be revered in Quaker circles. But Connie disliked the idea of idolizing her husband as some kind of prophet; he was more complex, more human, and more fun than that, she felt. The character sketch provided by his cousin Joshua Rowntree preceding a posthumous collection of John's thought, *Essays and Addresses*, bears this out, as it traces his transformation from an occasionally violent-tempered youth to a man admired for his gentleness and understanding. So how did he change? His physical and spiritual suffering seems to have played a role. According to an article in *The Friend*, 'He had found the solution of the problem of suffering in the revelation of a suffering God, and his conscious realisation of the love of Christ in his own heart came to him when he had entered into the fellowship of His sufferings. And so there was something about his ministry both in public worship and personal intercourse, peculiarly comforting to all who mourned, or were in anxiety or distress.'[18] The result, as T. E. Harvey eloquently attested, was that 'To him a man could open out his mind and lay bare his difficulties as to no other friend, and he who had gone through the gloomy sea of doubt was able to reach out a saving hand to those who felt themselves alone amid the waters'.[19]

In addition to the role of suffering, John talked of the effort involved in transformation. It was undeniably hard to resist the urge to respond sharply to an insult, he admitted, and to return instead a soft answer. In any case, restraint was not enough: he wanted not just to 'lop off' undesirable behaviour but to grow spiritually, to attain not only discipline but also victory. To do this, it was not enough to admire Christ. Prayer was key: 'By prayer, the prayer of our whole nature, voicing our abasement and our hope, our weakness and the strength of our striving, our unfitness and our longing, prayer that rises from the very depths of our being, such prayer alone can pierce the darkness that walls us round, and yield us the joy of the Divine illumination.'[20] E. T. W. Dennis wrote of what it was like to have John pray for him: 'Twas the cry of the child, with the child's faith, and the child's love; and so he led me, hand in hand, and then he spoke for me to God ... and as the words came a new strength came too, and a joy that seemed to have been either unknown, or forgotten, until he prayed.'[21]

This ability to embrace suffering, to study and to pray did not make John po-faced though. So the final word goes to Rufus Jones: 'He thoroughly enjoyed life and his happy spirit flowed out in sheer joy. He was full of good stories which he told with striking effect, and one could hardly believe that this man, weighted with his sense of mission and constantly facing the breakdown of his powers, could be so gay and so full of humor.'[22]

Chapter 7

The Quaker chocolate legacy

The three Quaker 'cocoa families' undoubtedly made huge contributions both in chocolate manufacturing and in society more widely. We've seen the reforms instigated by George and Richard Cadbury and Joseph Rowntree in conditions for factory workers, the tumultuous life of Beatrice Cadbury that questioned capitalism and promoted pacifism, and the bold and visionary changes that John Wilhelm Rowntree instigated within Quakerism in the face of a progressive disease. Other notable family members have been mentioned in passing, such as Arnold Rowntree, who was elected MP for York in 1910, and the war hero Bertie Cadbury. More recently, in 1991, Adrian Cadbury chaired the Committee on Financial Aspects of Corporate Governance, seeking to establish a code of best practices. Although Quaker values were not explicitly mentioned in the Cadbury Code, Adrian explained that its aim was to bring greater transparency, honesty, simplicity, and integrity to the process of running a company.

Both the Cadburys and the Rowntrees established trusts, and the Rowntree ones, in particular, are still very active, although they have changed slightly since their inception. The *Joseph Rowntree Foundation* (www.jrf.org.uk) aims to end poverty in the UK. The Foundation views ensuring dignity and respect for everyone as a moral cause and carries out policy work, research, and campaigns. The *Joseph Rowntree Reform Trust Ltd* (www.jrrt.org.uk) is a non-charitable trust that offers grants for political, campaigning, or lobbying purposes that are ineligible for charitable funding. It has a long-standing interest in backing activists defending civil liberties and striving for positive political change and democratic reform. The *Joseph Rowntree*

Charitable Trust (www.jrct.org.uk) supports those who address the root causes of conflict and injustice and who are tackling the climate crisis.

When it comes to chocolate itself, it seems that many of the issues that the Quaker cocoa families wrestled with remain. One of the most pressing is the labour conditions on cacao plantations. We saw that William Cadbury made strenuous efforts to halt the bonded labour instigated by the Portuguese in Angola, and that the Quakers decided to continue using cacao produced in this way in the hope of being able to use the leverage that came with being a major buyer. Not everyone agreed with their decision, but the *Times* seemed to acknowledge the complexities of the case, writing that 'It would always be a nice question for moralists what should be done in the circumstances revealed by this trial'.[1]

Today, the Joseph Rowntree trusts recognize that they benefited from shareholdings in a company that made profits deriving from the purchase of raw materials from enslaved people. A statement issued in April 2021 acknowledges that 'We are deeply sorry that the origins of our endowment have roots in shameful practices that caused deep suffering and created enduring harms'.[2] They have committed both to investigating this part of their history more fully and to making reparation, realizing that they cannot truly be an anti-poverty organization unless they are also an anti-racist organization.

Human rights abuses in the cacao industry are still depressingly widespread, however.[3] Recent investigations report millions of farmers subsisting on less than $1 a day, and children wielding machetes and spraying toxic agrochemicals instead of attending school: an estimated 1.5 million children work in Ghana and the Ivory Coast alone. From an industry perspective, campaigners have argued that the solution lies partly in better governance from both chocolate-consuming and cacao-producing nations. Supply management needs to be improved and regulations put in place such that companies pay higher prices and offer long-term contracts to provide farmers with financial security. The scale of the problem is clearly huge, but various organizations are trying to improve the situation. The World Cocoa Foundation (www.worldcocoafoundation. org), for example, draws its membership from farmer cooperatives, cocoa processors, chocolate manufacturers, and supply chain companies and aims to make the cocoa sector fair and sustainable. The VOICE Network (www.voicenetwork.cc) is a global network of NGOs and trade unions that acts as a watchdog and catalyst for a reformed cocoa sector. It publishes the biennial *The Cocoa Barometer*, which aims to provide a clear overview of the state of sustainability.

From the consumer's perspective, most of us are familiar with the Fairtrade initiative to address poor working conditions and low pay. The first Fairtrade-certified chocolate bar in the UK was Green & Black's Maya Gold, in 1994. The company, founded by Jo Fairley, offered a guaranteed fair price for cacao grown without fertilizers and pesticides, enabling Maya farmers in Belize to send their children to school and afford medical care. Fairtrade has certainly improved conditions for many farmers and may ease our conscience. Not surprisingly, however, the complexities of life and commerce mean that the system is not infallible. A lack of resources means that farms are not always audited thoroughly, and it is not always the case that the Fairtrade premium reaches the farmer: sometimes it finds a home with middlemen. Furthermore, the Scottish philosopher William MacAskill, known for his work on effective giving, casts some doubt on the concept itself. Discussing Fairtrade in the coffee industry, he points out that because Fairtrade standards are difficult to meet, the very poorest countries cannot afford certification. He concludes that as consumers we could do considerably more good by buying cheaper goods and donating the money saved to a cost-effective charity.[4]

A further issue relates to the health benefits of cacao on the one hand and the harms caused by mass-produced chocolate on the other. Back in the 1750s, recall, Joseph Fry was selling chocolate as an oily health drink in his Bristol apothecary. Today, as the health benefits of cacao have been investigated, it is once more possible to buy cacao in pharmacies, but now in capsule form. The basis of the health claims is that, as a plant, cacao is rich in polyphenols. These chemicals are produced by plants to protect against environmental effects such as predators or harsh conditions, and they have been shown to have health benefits arising from their antioxidant and anti-inflammatory properties.

Research into the health benefits of chocolate is still patchy, however. A review paper in 2019 summarized some of the findings, but with the caveat that studies were scarce, that there was a big difference between cacao and mass-produced chocolate (e.g., because cacao loses some of its polyphenols during processing), and that confounding factors such as overall diet and lifestyle might have affected the results.[5] That said, there were some encouraging findings for chocolate lovers. Chocolate was linked with reduced cardiovascular risk (but one study suggested that the ideal dose was a paltry 45 g per week), a decreased risk of stroke, and the prevention of diabetes (although the presence of sugar in mass-produced chocolate may counteract this benefit). The picture in relation to cancer is unclear: some laboratory studies showed that cacao inhibited the growth of cancer cells, but other studies suggested that excess chocolate intake could increase the risk of colorectal and breast cancer. Regarding the immune system, some studies showed that it had a positive effect, while others showed that it was associated with hypersensitivity reactions, manifesting as fatigue, irritability, headaches, etc. Other studies have shown that it reduces the risk of cognitive decline, and that it does indeed act as an aphrodisiac. The good news for teens is that it has been shown that chocolate does *not* cause acne.

There is also the complication from additives. We saw how Cadbury, in particular, took pride in their cocoa being 'absolutely pure, therefore best', while other manufacturers added fats and starches. Today, the ingredient list for a typical mass-produced chocolate bar includes sugar, cocoa butter, cocoa mass, vegetable fats (palm, shea), emulsifiers (E442, E476), and flavouring. Clearly, the added sugar contributes to obesity and tooth decay (one can imagine the dismay that George Cadbury and Joseph Rowntree would have felt, given their efforts to improve childhood and dental health), although this needs to be seen in the wider matrix of cultural ideas about the desirability of chocolate, advertising, and supermarket product placement. The emulsifiers and fats are widely used as a cheap alternative to extra cacao butter, and the flavourings are factory-produced to give a consistent flavour to a product that naturally would vary depending on the particular harvest and origin of the beans. Artisan plain chocolate, by contrast, generally has three ingredients: whole cacao beans, organic sugar, and organic cacao butter, and the flavour will vary from batch to batch. It is more expensive but will have greater health benefits.

Finally, one issue that has emerged since the Quaker chocolate heyday is the environmental damage associated with cacao production.[6] Organizations such as the Rainforest Alliance, with its frog logo, aim to support social, economic, and environmental sustainability for various commodities, including chocolate. But the global chocolate trade is worth more than $1trillion a year, so the scale of the task and the undeniable financial needs of small-scale, poor farmers mean that the problems are widespread and complex. The ecological degradation associated with the palm oil that is added to chocolate has been well publicized, especially regarding the destruction of the habitat of orangutans, but cacao, too, is associated with soil erosion, forest destruction, and the misuse of fertilizer. A recent survey of the Ivory Coast using satellite imagery, for example, found that cacao was being grown on nearly 14 per cent of the country's protected areas.

The history of chocolate has taken us from human sacrifice, through royal courts, to modern factories, and the ethical issues surrounding it have ranged from additives to slavery. British Quakers played a key role in developing mass production and in improving the lives of their employees. They may not be directly involved in chocolate manufacturing today, but the Quaker testimonies of integrity, equality, community, and environmental stewardship surely have a role to play in its future.

Notes

Introduction
1.   The terms cacoa/cocoa/chocolate are often used interchangeably in books and articles about chocolate. I have generally followed the convention of using 'cacoa' for the unprocessed form, 'cocoa' for the powder used to make a drink, and 'chocolate' for solid bars.

Chapter 1
1.   S. D. Coe & M. D. Coe, *The True History of Chocolate* (Thames & Hudson, 2019), 82.
2.   Coe & Coe, *True History*, 114.
3.   P. Chrystal, *Rowntrees: The Early History* (Pen & Sword, 2021), 37.
4.   Coe & Coe, *True History*, 166.
5.   Coe & Coe, *True History*, 205.
6.   G. Wagner, *The Chocolate Conscience* (Chatto & Windus, 1987), 10.
7.   Wagner, *Chocolate Conscience*, 13.

Chapter 2
1.   Wagner, *Chocolate Conscience*, 21.
2.   Yearly Meeting is a term that describes both a body of Quakers that are members of local meetings, and the annual event at which these Quakers meet up.
3.   D. Cadbury, *Chocolate Wars* (Public Affairs, 2010), 12.
4.   A. C. Gardiner, *Life of George Cadbury* (Cassell & Co., 1923), 311.
5.   Cadbury, *Chocolate Wars*, 62.
6.   Gardiner, *George Cadbury*, 36.
7.   I. Carrington, *Cadbury's Angels* (Monks Bridge Books, 2011), 66.

8. Cadbury, *Chocolate Wars*, 197.
9. A. Vernon, *A Quaker Business Man: The Life of Joseph Rowntree* (Sessions Book Trust, 1987), 81.
10. Chrystal, *Rowntrees*, 27.

Chapter 3

1. Gardiner, *George Cadbury*, 25.
2. Carrington, *Cadbury's Angels*, 18.
3. Cadbury, *Chocolate Wars*, 104.
4. Gardiner, *George Cadbury*, 29.
5. Carrington, *Cadbury's Angels*, 40.
6. Cadbury, *Chocolate Wars*, 121.
7. Gardiner, *George Cadbury*, 31.
8. Carrington, *Cadbury's* Angels, 44.
9. Gardiner, *George Cadbury*, 117.
10. Wagner, *Chocolate Conscience*, 152.
11. Gardiner, *George Cadbury*, 117.
12. Gardiner, *George Cadbury*, 231.
13. Gardiner, *George Cadbury*, 234.
14. Gardiner, *George Cadbury*, 254.
15. Gardiner, *George Cadbury*, 199.
16. Gardiner, *George Cadbury*, 75.
17. Carrington, *Cadbury's Angels*, 137.
18. Gardiner, *George Cadbury*, 50.
19. Cadbury, *Chocolate Wars*, 228.

Chapter 4

1. Vernon, *Quaker Business Man*, 33.
2. Vernon, *Quaker Business Man*, 18.
3. Vernon, *Quaker Business Man*, 40.
4. Vernon, *Quaker Business Man*, 41.
5. Chrystal, *Rowntrees*, 112.
6. Vernon, *Quaker Business Man*, 63.
7. Chrystal, *Rowntrees*, 97.

8. Cadbury, *Chocolate Wars*, 69.
9. Chrystal, *Rowntrees*, 127.
10. Chrystal, *Rowntrees*, 137,
11. Vernon, *Quaker Business Man*, 127.
12. Vernon, *Quaker Business Man*, 147.
13. Vernon, *Quaker Business Man*, 153.
14. C. Titley, *Joseph Rowntree* (Shire, 2013), 6.
15. Vernon, *Quaker Business Man*, 157.
16. Titley, *Jospeh Rowntree*, 33.
17. Vernon, *Quaker Business Man*, 110.
18. Titley, *Jospeh Rowntree*, 55.
19. Wagner, *Chocolate Conscience*, 65.

Chapter 5
1. F. Jospeh, *Beatrice: The Cadbury Heiress Who Gave Away Her Fortune* (Foxwell Press, 2012), 54.
2. Joseph, *Beatrice*, 53.
3. Joseph, *Beatrice*, 58.
4. Joseph, *Beatrice*, 76.
5. Joseph, *Beatrice*, 83.

Chapter 6
1. S. Allott, *John Wilhelm Rowntree* (Sessions Book Trust, 1994), viii.
2. Titley, *Joseph Rowntree*, 33.
3. J. Rowntree (ed.) *John Wilhelm Rowntree: Essays and Addresses* (Headley Brothers, 1905), xi.
4. Rowntree, *Essays and Addresses*, xii.
5. Society of Friends, *Report of the Proceedings of the Conference in Manchester* (Headley Brothers, 1895), 383–384.
6. Rowntree, *Essays and Addresses*, xvii.
7. Rowntree, *Essays and Addresses*, xxiv.
8. Rowntree, *Essays and Addresses*, xviii.

9. R. Jones, *John Wilhelm Rowntree* (Friends General Conference, 1942), unpaginated.

10. Allott, *John Wilhelm Rowntree*, 35.

11. Society of Friends, *Manchester*, 31.

12. Society of Friends, *Manchester*, 75–82.

13. E. Vining, *Friend of Life: The Biography of Rufus M. Jones* (J. B. Lippincott, 1958), 72.

14. Vining, *Friend of Life*, 98.

15. Chrystal, *Rowntrees*, 154.

16. Letter from Joan Fry, Rufus Jones Special Collection, Haverford College, Box 9.

17. Vining, *Friend of Life*, 112.

18. Rowntree, *Essays and Addresses*, xxix.

19. Rowntree, *Essays and Addresses*, xxx.

20. Allott, *John Wilhelm Rowntree*, 67.

21. Rowntree, *Essays and Addresses*, xxx.

22. Jones, *John Wilhelm Rowntree*, unpaginated.

Chapter 7

1. Wagner, *Chocolate Conscience*, 102.

2. https://www.jrf.org.uk/press/statement-joseph-rowntree-foundation-jrf-trustees-and-joseph-rowntree-housing-trust-jrht-board.

3. See e.g. https://www.theguardian.com/environment/2023/jan/21/chocolate-ethical-affordable-fair-trade; https://www.theguardian.com/global-development/2020/oct/20/chocolate-industry-slammed-for-failure-to-crack-down-on-child-labour.

4. W. MacAskill, *Doing Good Better* (Guardian Books, 2015), 164–167.

5. M. T. Montagna et al. 'Chocolate, "Food of the Gods": History, Science, and Human Health'. *International Journal of Environmental Research and Public Health*, 2019; 16(24): 4960.

6.   www.theguardian.com/environment/2023/may/22/cocoa-planting-is-destroying-protected-forests-in-west-africa-study-finds.

Further reading

Allott, S. *John Wilhelm Rowntree* (Sessions Book Trust, 1994).

Cadbury, D. *Chocolate Wars* (PublicAffairs, 2010).

Carrington, I. *Cadbury's Angels: Memories of Working with George Cadbury from Bridge Street to Bournville* (Monks Bridge Books, 2011).

Chrystal, P. *Rowntrees: The Early History* (Pen & Sword, 2021).

Coe, S. D. & Coe, M. D. *The True History of Chocolate* (Thames & Hudson, 2019).

Gardiner, A. C. *Life of George Cadbury* (Cassell & Co., 1923).

Jones, R. M. *John Wilhelm Rowntree* (Friends General Conference, 1942).

Joseph, F. *Beatrice: The Cadbury Heiress Who Gave Away Her Fortune* (Foxwell Press, 2012).

MacAskill, W. *Doing Good Better* (Guardian Books, 2015).

Rowntree, J. (ed.) *John Wilhelm Rowntree: Essays and Addresses* (Headley Brothers, 1905).

Society of Friends *Report of the Proceedings of the Conference in Manchester* (Headley Brothers, 1895).

Stranz, W. *George Cadbury* (Shire, 1973).

Titley, C. *Joseph Rowntree* (Shire, 2013).

Vernon, A. *A Quaker Business Man: The Life of Joseph Rowntree* (Sessions Book Trust: York, 1987).

Vining, E. G. *Friend of Life: The Biography of Rufus M. Jones* (J. B. Lippincott, 1958).

Wagner, G. *The Chocolate Conscience* (Chatto & Windus, 1987).

For information on the Rowntree family, company, and trusts, see https://www.rowntreesociety.org.uk/

CHRISTIAN ALTERNATIVE
BOOKS

THE NEW OPEN SPACES

Throughout the two thousand years of Christian tradition
there have been, and still are, groups and individuals
that exist in the margins and upon the edge of faith. But
in Christianity's contrapuntal history it has often been
these outcasts and pioneers that have forged contemporary
orthodoxy out of former radicalism as belief evolves to engage
with and encompass the ever-changing social and scientific
realities. Real faith lies not in the comfortable certainties of
the Orthodox, but somewhere in a half-glimpsed hinterland
on the dirt track to Emmaus, where the Death of God meets
the Resurrection, where the supernatural Christ meets the
historical Jesus, and where the revolution liberates
both the oppressed and the oppressors.

Welcome to Christian Alternative... a space at the
edge where the light shines through.
If you have enjoyed this book, why not tell other readers
by posting a review on your preferred book site.

Recent bestsellers from Christian Alternative are:

Bread Not Stones
The Autobiography of An Eventful Life
Una Kroll
The spiritual autobiography of a truly remarkable
woman and a history of the struggle for ordination in the
Church of England.
Paperback: 978-1-78279-804-0 ebook: 978-1-78279-805-7

The Quaker Way
A Rediscovery
Rex Ambler
Although fairly well known, Quakerism is not well
understood. The purpose of this book is to explain how
Quakerism works as a spiritual practice.
Paperback: 978-1-78099-657-8 ebook: 978-1-78099-658-5

Blue Sky God
The Evolution of Science and Christianity
Don MacGregor
Quantum consciousness, morphic fields and blue-sky
thinking about God and Jesus the Christ.
Paperback: 978-1-84694-937-1 ebook: 978-1-84694-938-8

Celtic Wheel of the Year
Tess Ward
An original and inspiring selection of prayers combining
Christian and Celtic Pagan traditions, and interweaving
their calendars into a single pattern of prayer for
every morning and night of the year.
Paperback: 978-1-90504-795-6

Christian Atheist
Belonging without Believing
Brian Mountford
Christian Atheists don't believe in God but miss him:
especially the transcendent beauty of his music,
language, ethics, and community.
Paperback: 978-1-84694-439-0 ebook: 978-1-84694-929-6

Compassion Or Apocalypse?
A Comprehensible Guide to the Thoughts of René Girard
James Warren
How René Girard changes the way we think about
God and the Bible, and its relevance for our
apocalypse-threatened world.
Paperback: 978-1-78279-073-0 ebook: 978-1-78279-072-3

Diary Of A Gay Priest
The Tightrope Walker
Rev. Dr. Malcolm Johnson
Full of anecdotes and amusing stories, but the Church
is still a dangerous place for a gay priest.
Paperback: 978-1-78279-002-0 ebook: 978-1-78099-999-9

Readers of ebooks can buy or view any of these bestsellers by
clicking on the live link in the title. Most titles are published in
paperback and as an ebook. Paperbacks are available
in traditional bookshops. Both print and ebook
formats are available online.

Find more titles and sign up to our readers' newsletter at
www.collectiveinkbooks.com/christianity Follow us on
Facebook at https://www.facebook.com/ChristianAlternative

Also in this series

Quaker Quicks - In Search of Stillness
Using a simple meditation to find inner peace
Joanna Godfrey Wood
ISBN: 978-1-78904-707-3

PGIL2024USA